18: PERSPECTIVES IN CRITICISM

PERSPECTIVES IN CRITICISM

18:

William E. Baker

Syntax in
English Poetry
1870-1930

UNIVERSITY OF CALIFORNIA PRESS
Berkeley and Los Angeles
1967

University of California Press
Berkeley and Los Angeles, California
Cambridge University Press
London, England

LIBRARY OF CONGRESS CATALOG CARD NO. 67-64721
Printed in the United States of America

For Pat, Willa, and Jo

Acknowledgments

I WISH to thank Miss Josephine Miles of the University of California for her astute comments on this manuscript, and for encouragement in its preparation. I am also grateful to the following persons and publishers for permission to quote copyrighted materials:

William Blackwood and Sons, Ltd. for quotations from "A Farewell to Naples" in *Blackwood's Magazine*, Vol. LXVII, No. 412, Feb. 1850.

City Lights Books for quotations from Allen Ginsberg's "Howl" in *Howl and Other Poems*, copyright 1956 and 1959 by Allen Ginsberg.

Collins-Knowlton-Wing, Inc. and A. P. Watt and Son for quotations from Robert Graves' "Halls of Bedlam" in *Collected Poems 1955*, copyright 1955 by Robert Graves.

Harcourt, Brace and World for quotations from E. E. Cummings' "W," "Is 5," "It started when Bill's chip let on to," in *Collected Poems*, copyright 1963 by Harcourt, Brace and World, and for "helves surling out of eakspeasies per (reel) hapsingly" in *Poems 1923–1954*, copyright 1931 and 1959 by E. E. Cummings; to Harcourt, Brace and World and to Faber and Faber, Ltd. for quotations from T. S. Eliot's "The Wasteland" in *Collected Poems 1909–1962*, copyright 1936 by Harcourt, Brace and World, copyright 1963, 1964 by T. S. Eliot; for quotations from Carl Sandburg's "Slabs of the Sunburnt West" in *Complete Poems*, copyright 1950 by Harcourt, Brace and World.

Contents

Introduction

IN THE LAST FEW YEARS, scholars devoted to literary studies have become more and more interested in the work of modern linguists. Aside from sporadic residual hostility toward scientism in the humanities, there seems to be general agreement that close examination of the verbal structure of poetry and fiction can only profit students of literature; and the linguist has for some time been willing to grant that as long as poets keep experimenting no grammarian is safe in ignoring them. Such, at any rate, was the conclusion of eminent scholars in both disciplines at a now famous "conference on style" held at the University of Indiana in 1958. Roman Jakobson summed up that conference: "All of us here . . . definitely realize that a linguist deaf to the poetic function of language and a literary scholar indifferent to linguistic problems and unconversant with linguistic methods are equally flagrant anachronisms." [1]

This mutual awareness augurs well for future studies in "stylistics," but so far efforts at cross-disciplinary scholarship have not been as satisfying as many had hoped. This remains true despite a number of shared fundamental assumptions, primarily, that poetry manifests licenses and restrictions not evident in other uses of the language. Nevertheless, poetry is a part of the whole language; and, therefore, what we can learn about language can help us understand literature, and vice versa. Yet the linguist still feels uncomfortable

1

talking about the "meaning" of discourse (unless he refers to the purely formal meaning of morphological or syntactic signals); while, if he becomes too deeply preoccupied with the mere mechanics of language, the literary man begins to feel guilty of murdering to dissect, or fears that E. E. Cummings' charge against those "who pay attention to the syntax of things" indeed applies to him, and that he must make a choice between experiencing the most profound human passions and mastering the fundamentals of Immediate Constituent analysis. In both cases, what may appear at first to be irrational fears are in fact healthy intuitions of some fundamental differences between the linguist's approach to language and the literary critic's approach to poetry.

We can contrast these differences most strikingly if we pause to consider how specialists in these two fields approach a text or a "speech event" or a "linguistic occurrence"—what someone writes or says. The linguist observes this use of the language and describes it in detailed form in order to compare it analytically with other uses of the language; he may then construct a grammar which is both a systematic description of the way the language commonly functions and a set of formulae to generate other sequences in perfect accord with the grammar. A literary critic or historian of literature, on the other hand, first *responds* to a work of art, likes or dislikes it, and only then seeks to isolate those specific characteristics of diction, rhythm, structure, or euphony which provoked his response; almost invariably he discovers (1) that those significant characteristics are *deviations* from the language as it commonly functions and (2) that, however accurately it may distinguish one author from another, a mere list of these peculiarities of style cannot adequately "explain" his response, which depends on a complex interplay of those distinctive features and his own consciousness. Consequently, the critic interprets the work only partly in terms of its objective features. In the end he must evaluate his response to a text in the light of his whole history of responses to other works of literature. Thus, in the one case, the product of research is a neutral grammar, a highly abstract system capable of producing a large number of "correct" sentences of equivalent merit; in the other case the product of research is a hierarchy of concrete verbal structures which does not automatically produce new structures and cannot even claim to justify beyond question its own configuration. The hierarchy may in fact reshuffle itself to a greater or lesser degree with each new inclusion.

It is also apparent that the linguist's inductive method is quite unlike the literary critic's reliance on his own sensitivity as the principle of selection and the directive force in a scholarly inquiry. Of the important steps in linguistic science—*observing, describing, comparing, constructing,* and *generating*—only the first three are relevant to literary study, and they become relevant not as the foundation and beginning of such study, but only after the most important decisions have been made. The critic can hardly avoid beginning his study of a text by reading it, and as soon as he reads he responds, that is, he evaluates. To confirm or reject that judgment, he may indeed have recourse to painstaking description of the work and subsequent careful comparison of it to other works. He seeks not to derive general rules, however, but to discover the effect of unique variations, from the subtle to the outlandish. And the fact remains that his first tentative evaluation of the work as worthy of thorough study is primary and crucial; the interpretation which follows then subjects that evaluation to continuous review and revision. For when a critic "interprets" a poem, he does not simply explain what it means; he tries to bring empirical analysis and subjective response into definite and meaningful relation to each other.

The following study approaches style largely from the literary viewpoint. It has been assumed, a priori,

3

that the poetry analyzed is worth reading just because it affects the reader in an unusual way, just because "The Windhover" stimulates us more than 14 lines from the telephone directory. Likewise, it is taken for granted that an individual poet's organization of language is partly responsible for these unusual effects. This latter assumption is widely shared, I think, by students of literature. It is not so easy, however, to arrive at a viable method of testing it or proceeding beyond it. To say that something called "poetic effect" is dependent upon style is one thing; to demonstrate just how this is so is quite another. Here the linguist's preoccupation with precise description and analytic comparison can serve as an instructive example. The man of letters is often adept at rendering for others his subtle, inner response to a work; he as often does not so carefully delineate the objective form of the poet's language. I have therefore laid great stress on the mechanics of language (without, however, any pretentions to having mastered the vocabulary of linguistic science); I have unashamedly tried to quantify stylistic characteristics; I have even analyzed parts of poems without reference to the whole. The aim was not to amass this data for its own sake, but for the light it might shed on those primary, intuitive responses to the language of great poets. Understanding the connection between features of style and affective power depends, surely, on a precise delineation of both.

Doubtless the necessary degree of precision cannot be reached until catholic men of letters, trained in both literature and linguistics, elaborate a common vocabulary and a general theory of style—a theory with principles more substantial than "style is the man" and more suggestive than the proposition that style is a "message" transmitted by the distribution and frequency of linguistic elements and their "transitional probabilities." Such a theory should have both synchronic and diachronic dimensions, and it should easily integrate the

4

most detailed examinations of the language of individual poets into generalizations about period style. It could, finally, integrate these generalizations into a systematic account of the whole language, which has in turn its relation to culture and historical process. Modern linguistics again provides us with a model: for example, the work of Chomsky, Harris (et al.), refining a rigorous structural description of language from phoneme to finished sentence, and M. A. K. Halliday's sketch of a unified theory of grammar could furnish at least the notion of a theory and method to account for the special grammar of poetry.[2] Some writers have already made exploratory studies along these lines.[3] In the pages that follow I have made no attempt to accomplish so exalted a goal; I have merely tried to analyze one major feature of style—syntax—in selections of poetry from a limited period of time, and to relate that analysis to accompanying subjective responses.

To be sure, one risks falling between two stools. Neither the scientific linguist nor the critic relying chiefly on a refined sensibility is likely to be happy with this approach. The former will find the terminology obsolete and the definitions unacceptably flexible; the latter will object to the counting of lines that deserve to be savored. But both, hopefully, will be irritated because the study falls short of their expectations, not because it was wrongheaded to begin with.

This inquiry restricts itself to syntax in poetry for two related reasons: (1) During the nineteenth century and the first decades of the twentieth, literary scholars discussed word order only indirectly, in its relation to prosody, rhyme scheme, and genre;[4] but since the appearance of "modern" verse forms, it is difficult to make precise observations about poems in these traditional terms. A great many modern poems have no definite metrical pattern or rhyme scheme and belong to no genre other than the loose one of "free verse." (2) Studies of poetic language in the last 25 years or so have therefore been less concerned with the formal musical properties of verse than with diction: recurrent images, continuity and variation in vocabulary between generations of poets, and the structure of verbal ambiguities and associations in a poem. While much of this work is accurate and comprehensive, serving both to characterize the style of individual authors and to fill in the history of poetic fashions,[5] it needs to be supplemented by an account of the patterning of language in poetry. Much of the commentary on this latter aspect of style remains either sketchy or too general and imprecise.[6]

Very few writers have discussed the syntax of poetry in detail,[7] though surely the disposition of words and phrases in verse helps determine style.[8] In modern poetry, like the work of Eliot, Lawrence, and Sandburg, rhyme is so often absent, structure so loose, and metrical pattern so problematical that to study such poetry closely one is almost forced to consider its syntax; that is, the way the words are put together. But when a literary critic discusses syntax his remarks are usually brief, general, and thinly substantiated. There are a few exceptions. One recent book on the subject, Donald Davie's *Articulate Energy*, contains sound and original insights; but Davie has attempted primarily to expose the virtues and inadequacies of current poetic theories of syntax.[9] He has recognized the agrammatical character of modern poetry, but has illustrated only briefly this unorthodoxy. And his insights are expressed figuratively rather than definitively, as the title of the book and the titles of some subchapters ("Syntax Like Music," "Syntax Like Mathematics") suggest. There are also extensive studies of selected grammatical devices in poetry (G. R. Hamilton's *The Tell-Tale Article*, Christine Brooke-Rose's *Grammar of Metaphor*, and Francis Berry's *Poet's Grammar*),[10] but none of these deals systematically and thoroughly with syntax in poetry as distinct from semantics and morphology.

6

Berry, for example, restricts himself to person, tense, and mood. Brooke-Rose studies intensively only certain constructions allied with figurative language: possessives, the copula joining two nouns, and so forth. In short, students of literature have not yet defined in any detail the function of syntax in poetry.

Linguists, on the other hand, now and then examine poetry with a perhaps obsessive concern for strict definition. Samuel Levin, in a monograph, elaborates painstakingly a technical vocabulary with which to attack lines from Shakespeare and Alexander Pope.[11] He discovers in these poets a phenomenon that he labels "coupling" and concludes that the phenomenon, which involves seeking "equivalences" in the "semantic" and "general phonetico-physiological continuum[s]," is "important for poetry" because it restricts one's choice of words.

The average reader, if he weathers this encounter with scientific diction, will grasp that Levin is only saying that to make sense in rhymed couplets of balanced, parallel structure requires of the poet a special effort. Empirical corroboration of a commonplace is, of course, welcome but of limited value. In a review of Levin's monograph, Nicolas Ruwet properly observes that its value lies in the application, largely successful, of a general hypothesis about style to a quite specific case.[12] Ruwet himself proceeds to expand Levin's remarks to include more complex interrelations between syntax, phonology, and semantic associations, and arrives at a rather thorough and sophisticated account of the functional structure of two of Louise Labé's sonnets. But these investigations, like a number of others involving the application of linguistic science to problems of metrics and phonetic patterning, treat poetry written according to traditional conventions of the art—conventions that are often absent from twentieth century poetry.[13]

Criticism of unconventional modern poetry suffers

especially from a divorce of careful analysis from happy insight. In journals we find the exhaustive documentation of details and in books the headiest of educated speculation. Seldom can we trace the growth of the one out of the other. Criticism of wide scope is especially baffling in its vagueness. During the last three decades, writers like Wallace Fowlie, Frederick Pottle, and Herbert Read have spoken of modern verse as "pure" poetry, a "mandarin" language; [14] or like Louise Bogan they stress "the complex and evasive spirit of modernity," [15] or the "modern sensibility" which expresses "intense feeling by oblique means." [16] In a similar vein Elizabeth Drew contrasts the "too facile and superficial technique of the Victorians" with the "oblique approach" of Eliot and Pound.[17] Babette Deutsch states that Pound is largely responsible for "the charged language that is the feature of poetry in our time;" [18] while J. Isaacs claims that the earmark of modern poetry is its "suggestive indefiniteness." [19] Occasionally critics are a little more specific: 30 years ago Eliot mentioned that to write "difficult" and "indirect" verse one must "dislocate" language,[20] and John Crowe Ransom likewise believes that the difficulty of modern poetry is due in part to "syntactic displacement." [21] Robinson Jeffers hints as much when he criticizes contemporary writers for "unnatural metaphors, hiatuses, and labored obscurity." [22] John Press, in *The Chequer'd Shade*, attempted to identify the syntactic structures responsible for obscurity, remarking, "a poet's syntax is almost more important than his vocabulary," and "The fundamental importance of syntax in poetry has seldom been understood or even discussed by the majority of critics, who have preferred to meander through the more picturesque byways of poetic diction, although poets themselves have given due emphasis to this difficult aspect of their craft." [23]

Rarely, in the sort of criticism to which Press refers, does the reader find clearly identified the components

8

of a style, so that he may know its concrete configuration. Paraphrase and commentary are far more common than anatomy. Where very specific analysis does occur, it often serves only an immediate and limited purpose. It is true that extensive and accurate accounts of the language of Shakespeare, Jonson, Milton, Keats, Browning, Shaw, Yeats, and Eliot occur in books devoted to these authors, and that the new critics have undertaken laborious dissections of individual poems; but a synthesis of such accounts arriving at historical perspective has yet to be properly made. Numerous accounts of T. S. Eliot's poetry, for example, refer to what Helen Gardner calls his "unlimited linguistic daring." [24] Williamson refers to "elliptical phrasing" and "subtle rhythms"; Matthiessen mentions the poet's "irregular verse and difficult sentence structure." [25] But how, exactly, does this daring use of language manifest itself? How does a line of Eliot differ from one of Tennyson or Hardy? This study is an attempt to answer such questions by comparing certain traits of poetic syntax in two successive periods of literary history.

If these traits are carefully defined, the comparison will provide facts which may be helpful in relating a poet's language to the developing tradition of his art. The same facts may also tell us something about how an individual poet manages his effects, and about how a group of poets, living in the same age, develops a common idiom to respond to that age. Thus, although most of the emphasis here is upon clearly describing a change in style, the last chapters suggest, on the one hand, ways of connecting this change with a wider cultural context and, on the other hand, ways of applying syntactic analysis to the study of individual poets and individual poems. The shift from description to suggestion is, I trust, plainly marked.

9

1

Outline of Method

A STUDY OF LINES from two groups of poets sixty years apart shows that both groups wrote predominantly regular sentences; that is, sentences whose fundamental pattern is a familiar one in English. However, poets writing around 1930 habitually varied their syntax in certain ways different from poets writing around 1870. Late nineteenth-century poets consistently altered the normal pattern of English sentences by elaboration— adding lengthy clauses or numerous parallel modifiers —and by dislocation—arranging the fundamental units of a sentence in unusual sequences. Twentieth century poets have markedly preferred, along with a stronger emphasis on the ordinary sentences of everyday discourse, the use of fragments—usually noun phrases or clauses—not clearly related to any one sentence. Each of the 30 poets studied here uses all three of these variations from regular order, but in different proportions and often for different effects.

Victorian writers generally sought variety through artifices consonant with traditional grammar. Modern poets, on the other hand, often make calculated departures from the conventions of grammar, as their use of fragments suggests. Of course some "Victorian" poets like Whitman and Browning employ styles like those of more recent poets, while some "modern" poets like Yeats or E. A. Robinson rely greatly on traditional syntactic patterns. It is especially helpful to determine the function of syntax in modern poetry, because this poetry often seems to be designed to imitate the character of spontaneous speech, as in the dramatic monologue, or to rely on the reader's ability to recognize groups of words as images emerging from a certain "state of mind" or emotion but not yet integrated into a grammatical statement. The understanding and appreciation of such poetry depend upon a recognition of the ways by which syntactic structures achieve emotional or psychological coherence through grammatical unorthodoxy.

An attempt to discuss in terms of three simple characteristics the styles of many diverse poets runs the risk of excessive generalization. One may object that remarks about so vague a trait as dislocation, as it appears in a dozen poets, have no particular bearing on the reading of poetry. Throughout the following chapters, even where the intent is to show broad historical development, I have attempted to define syntactic traits more exactly by citing their specific uses in specific poems. For example, a few lines from Bryant illustrate the function of two common kinds of syntactic variation operating together:

> . . . white cottages were seen
> With rose-trees at the windows; barns from which
> Came loud and shrill the crowing of the cock;
> Pastures where rolled and neighed the lordly horse,
> And white flocks browsed and bleated.[1]

This sentence acts as almost pure description; it is really a list given formal structure, wherein the neutral passive "were seen," lacking any agent, is yoked with three subjects in the form of nouns with complex clausal modifiers. According to the definitions given in subsequent pages, this sentence would be classified as "elaborate" because of the number of verbs in subordinate clauses and "dislocated" in at least two places because some of these verbs precede their subjects. This elaboration by addition of subordinate clauses allows the poet to present a single scene in which definite events—the crowing of the cock, neighing of the horse, bleating of the sheep—take place simultaneously or in indeterminate sequence, and in which the order of their occurrence is subordinate to their grouping in a tableau. The dislocations, simple inversions, contribute a touch of pomp bordering, perhaps, on the ludicrous for readers at mid-twentieth century. These dislocations do not complicate the lines and do not confound a reader; they serve either to vary the expected sequence or to provide a desired rhythm.

This pattern of a weak main verb whose subjects, objects, or subordinate elements are highly elaborated and also displaced for the sake of variety or cadence or rhyme occurs fairly often in Bryant:

> Yet pure its waters—its shallows are bright
> With colored pebbles and sparkles of light,
> And clear the depths where its eddies play,
> And dimples deepen and whirl away,
> And the plane-tree's speckled arms o'ershoot
> The swifter current that mines its root,
> Through whose shifting leaves, as you walk the hill,
> The quivering glimmer of sun and rill,
> With a sudden flash on the eye is thrown,
> Like the ray that streams from the diamond stone.[2]

> Ha! feel ye not your fingers thrill,
> As o'er them, in the yellow grains,
> Glide the warm drops of blood that fill,
> For mortal strife, the warrior's veins;
> Such as, on Solferino's day,
> Slaked the brown sand and flowed away;—
> Flowed till the herds, on Mincio's brink
> Snuffed the red stream and feared to drink;—

Blood that in deeper pools shall lie,
On the sad earth, as time grows gray,
When men by deadlier arts shall die,
And deeper darkness blot the sky
Above the thundering fray. . . .[3]

In these two passages the poet aims at dramatic digression rather than at pure description, but the digressions proceed through clauses linked grammatically within the bounds of a sentence. Disparate material is unified by grammatical device.

This sort of variation characterizes not only Bryant's work, but much of the poetry selected from 15 authors writing in the latter half of the nineteenth century. Early twentieth-century poets developed quite different manners. A typical passage from Pound's *Cantos* presents simple description in the form of a series of fragments:

Seal sports in the spray-whited circles of cliff-wash
Sleek head, daughter of Lir
    eyes of Picasso
Under black fur-hood, lithe daughter of
    Ocean. . . .[4]

It is highly probable, but not absolutely certain, that "sports" is a verb rather than a noun. Such ambiguity occurs often in modern poetry. The absence of connectives, articles, and conventional punctuation also helps to make the passage an agrammatical structure, one whose parts are not differentiated and related by usual methods. Phrases group themselves by semantic linking, not by grammar.

However, the distinction between Victorian and modern styles can easily be overemphasized and lead to false groupings. An extreme form of the elaboration illustrated by the quoted lines from Bryant has a certain resemblance to Pound's method of accretion by fragments. The chapter on elaboration defines this resemblance. Also, some poets both Victorian and modern employ elaboration consistently, but to different ends; and fragmentation occurs throughout both eras, though its use varies. According to the chart in Appendix I, Whitman and Tennyson wrote proportionately about as many fragments as Pound did; and E. A. Robinson and Yeats elaborated sentences more often than most nineteenth-century poets did. The number of dislocations in poetry indeed declines markedly from Longfellow to D. H. Lawrence, but E. E. Cummings uses this device as often as most nineteenth-century poets. Cummings' dislocations are also, to be sure, of a unique kind. Poetic style does not change suddenly and universally over this 60-year period: an account of the fragment as a "modern" syntactic structure must begin with Whitman, Tennyson, and Browning; Yeats's work must be seen as imbued with structural principles widespread in the poetry of his predecessors.

Historical perspective is nevertheless implicit in the following chapters describing kinds of syntactic variations, for these chapters have been arranged to illustrate how one combination of such structures characterizes most late nineteenth-century poetry; and another, the poetry of the early twentieth century. To make as sharp a distinction as possible between the dominant Victorian and modern styles, I have chosen works clustered about two convenient dates, 1870 and 1930. Minor exceptions are a poem by Oscar Wilde dated 1886 and one of Sandburg's published in 1916; most of the other works selected were written within ten years of the boundary dates. A chart in Appendix I lists in the order of their birth dates the 30 poets whose works have been analyzed. The poets from Bryant to Wilde form one group, those from Yeats to Thomas another.

These poets have been chosen first of all because their works have been actively preserved; that is, schools

14

still force or encourage students to read them, and literary scholars continue to comment upon them. Secondly, they have all been acclaimed as serious, significant poets by their own contemporaries or their immediate successors, so that they may be said to have either reinforced or modified prevailing fashions. The poets selected are the following: writing around 1870—Browning, Tennyson, Arnold, Morris, Hopkins, Rossetti, Swinburne, Hardy, Wilde, Bryant, Emerson, Lowell, Longfellow, Whitman, and Dickinson; writing around 1930—Yeats, Pound, H. D., Eliot, Lawrence, Graves, Auden, Thomas, Robinson, Frost, Sandburg, Stevens, Williams, Cummings, and Crane.

It should be understood, that the term "modern poetry" refers throughout only to the work of the latter group during one decade, and "Victorian" or "nineteenth-century poetry" to certain poems of the former group written around 1870. Insofar as he finds these groups representative, the reader may widen the scope of the terms, as I have done by implication.

Nor is it possible to deal with all the poetry produced by these 30 writers. I have chosen enough poems from each to provide a sample of about 500 lines. Strictly dramatic poetry has been excluded, but the dramatic monologue, a very popular modern form, has been included. The selections are, however, supposed to sample the author's characteristic style rather than one he invents for an exotic persona. Thus, I took from Browning's *The Ring and the Book* those introductory lines that relate the poet's discovery of the old yellow book. Certain poetic forms obviously impose certain restrictions on style, but this problem cannot be entirely avoided. Principles of selection were invoked to make such conditions of form fairly constant and still allow for a range of technique: The samples were drawn from more than one poem of each author but, usually, from fewer than five poems. Except for the selection from Browning, only complete poems or complete sections of long poems were chosen. Bits of dialogue, quotations from another author, and lines in foreign languages were omitted from consideration. All genres which impose a rigid, traditional structure on the poet—sonnets, ballades, sestinas—were avoided in favor of pieces of similar length, 100–300 lines of from six to twelve syllables, and of flexible, indeterminate, or original form. Appendix II is a list of the poems by author comprising the sample.

Syntax itself is here defined simply as the ordering of words and word groups into a significant pattern. Let us avoid for the moment the question of to whom the words should be significant and concentrate on the concept of variations in the pattern of a language. In all that follows, the sentence is a pattern of maximum complexity, the word the simplest element in that pattern.[5] Since grammarians by no means agree on what a sentence is, one has some liberty in his choice of a definition.

For purposes of this study, an independent finite verb is considered the indispensable kernel of any sentence. The verb ordinarily functions among and with word groups related grammatically to it. Of these word groups, the subject and complement or object (of transitive verbs) supply in most cases necessary pieces of the pattern and are therefore called *fundamental* elements. The other elements—modifying words, phrases, and clauses—may be ordered about the principal ones with some flexibility, depending on their function. In general the irreducible skeleton of a sentence is the subject, verb, and complement in that order. To this skeleton could be appended an infinite number of other words and groups of words, as long as each of these new elements is related, either by position or by a grammatical connective, either to one of the fundamental elements or to another element ultimately related to a fundamental one.

Obviously, the number of possible arrangements of

16

these items is very great, but few recur enough to warrant attention. Here only four matter. One of these, the "norm," is called "regular" or "normal" because it resembles the structure of unpretentious prose and of everyday speech; the others—labeled "fragmentation," "elaboration," and "dislocation"—represent what are felt to be essential differences in the structure of a verbal expression. A sentence which contains only the essentials of subject and verb obviously differs from one which contains not only these essentials but a profusion of related words, and it differs also from a "structure" which, though apparently independent of any sentence, yet lacks a necessary element, usually a verb. And these three patterns differ from a fourth type in which words appear in an order seldom or never found in ordinary discourse. Thus, a variation from the regular pattern of a sentence occurs when words are added, deleted, or rearranged. Various further distinctions within these classifications have been drawn whenever they seem to have some significance in interpreting the poetry selected for the study.

Underlying this division into three categories of syntactic variation is a more fundamental principle of grammar. Any word or word group in a sentence can be said to have two distinct grammatical qualities: "character" and "location." [6] In the sentences "John loved Mary" and "Mary loved John," the noun "John" has in both cases the same character—the wordclass to which it belongs remains the same—but its location in the sentence and thus its grammatical function are different. In "John likes popcorn" and "John likes to swim," "popcorn" and "to swim" occupy the same location but have a different character, as is evident if we try to add "swiftly" to the ends of both sentences. These terms are the equivalents of but rather more immediately comprehensible than Sapir's "concrete concepts" and "relational concepts," or Hill's "language entities" in "recurrent designs," or Harris's "classes" and

17

"diagnostic co-occurents." [7] Some linguists would insist that character is *defined* by location, that we formulate a partial definition of a noun by stating that it is a word which can be preceded by "the" and followed by "is," but there is no need to pursue this chicken-and-egg argument. Once defined, words that function as nouns, verbs, adjectives, and so forth retain their grammatical character irrespective of context.

Thus a syntactic "dislocation" is defined as an alteration in the normal location of words or word groups, although radical dislocation may also introduce ambiguity about the character of some sentence element. "Elaboration" is a quantitative change in character, in that an extraordinary number of word groups with the same character function together in one sentence and often, though not necessarily, in the same location. "Fragmentation" is an unusual alteration in location; it occurs when a word or word group is without an orthodox location with respect to other words. And a "regular" sentence is, of course, a string of words of appropriate character in their customary locations.

Still, to define the regular sentence, one must depend in part on his intuition, or on someone's intuition. Modern linguists have fortunately agreed on certain sentence patterns as common, habitual, normal among the "native speakers" of a language. Usually the linguist, if he is also a native speaker, relies on his own usage, his "idiolect," as a standard of normality. I have followed this precedent to a degree, assembling corroboration from linguists when possible.

There is general accord that subject precedes verb; verb, object, with certain carefully defined exceptions. Bloomfield says simply that "the nominative expression precedes the finite verb expression." [8] Archibald Hill in his standard textbook of linguistics states, "The order subject-verb-complement is so normal and expected that we automatically interpret in accord with it and are more or less frustrated when we cannot." [9]

18

Noam Chomsky simply begins his analysis of grammar with a "rewrite" rule, $S \rightarrow Np + Vp$ (subject + verb) which presupposes the normality of this order.[10] And Charles Fries observes that the order of these fundamental elements determines large classifications of common sentence types in English, pointing out that verb-subject order occurs ordinarily only in questions or after certain negatives ("Never have we had any reason to question her honesty.") [11] Such inversions due to negation, however, I have counted as dislocations whenever they could be rephrased with at least equal idiomatic grace in normal order. Also, whereas Bloomfield considers "Yes," "What for?" and "Fire!" as types of sentences,[12] I have held all exclamations and responses, except for a plain "Yes" or "No" and the interjection "Alas," as fragmentary. The expression "O" or "Oh," common in poetry, I have ignored. With these few exceptions, the regular sentence can be defined simply as any sentence which does not contain one of the three variations, since these variations, though sometimes the rule with certain poets rather than the exception, are patterns found infrequently in utilitarian prose and common speech.

The fragment is perhaps easiest to recognize. Usually a verb disappears, as in such locutions as "Susy—a truly winsome girl," or "Time for chow," or "God's blood!" Poets have for a long time exercised the license of uttering exclamatory fragments (*O tempora, O mores!*), and colloquial expressions like "Why so pale" may also be fairly common in the history of English poetry. Exclamatory and colloquial fragments, therefore, have been recorded as subcategories within this primary mode of variation.

A certain kind of syntactic abnormality results when an unusual number of elements are joined to form a single sentence. This elaboration has been assigned a somewhat arbitrary value: sentences containing a minimum of five finite verbs, or one verb in an independent clause and three or more verbs in distinct subordinate clauses; and sentences with five compounded fundamental elements, or at least four modifying elements of identical grammatical function, have been catalogued as "elaborate" structures. Mere length of sentences seemed an insufficient criterion of complexity, whereas additional verbs or an extended series of modifiers acting in concert may not only amplify but also complicate thought. Two sentences of about equal length may differ exceedingly in the elaborateness of the relations they express. For example: (1) Appearing at the butcher shop on Christmas morning every year, his wizened face suffused with joy and gratitude, the old man received a fat goose from the townspeople. (2) Simply because he had known two kings before the other townspeople knew their own mothers, the old man got his Christmas goose, while younger, more useful men went hungry. This last kind of construction is not new in poetry. Blank verse especially, from Marlowe to Milton, achieved many of its rare effects through elaboration, the piling up of clause on clause on clause. Excessive elaboration, however, with its suggestion of the baroque, rarely belongs in the "normal" range of expression.

In dislocation, fundamental elements are shifted out of their standard order (subject + verb + object); or a modifying element is displaced from its normal position beside, or after, the element it modifies; or standard word order is interrupted by a parenthetical statement. English poets from Chaucer on have inverted fundamental elements to facilitate rhyme ("But on his brest a bloodie crosse he bore"). Such inversions are clearly stylistic innovations. Determining the normality of the disposition of modifiers, on the other hand, poses serious difficulties, for usage allows much flexibility in the positioning of some modifiers. For example, adverbs like "only" and "often" can occur almost anywhere in a sentence.

Following Fries and W. Nelson Francis, I hold the normal position of a one-word adjective to be before the noun,[13] and in addition maintain the normal position of prepositional phrases and participial adjectives with adverbial modifiers to be after the noun. Thus, "a day dark and dreary" and "the tossed by the waves ship" and "these from the smokehouse hams" are all dislocations. Similarly, at Hill's suggestion I consider adverbs formed by the -ly ending to be normally adjacent to the adjective they modify, so that "a task started by many hastily" would be a dislocation.[14] Finally, any complement preceding a copula ("In a mess he was") or any preposition preceding the verb with which it forms an idiomatic expression ("To Carthage then I came") or any adverbial phrase standing before an adjective ("The ship by the waves tossed") represents dislocation.

In practice the reader will find many more sorts of uncommon word order in any inventive poet, but a full description of such variations would be tediously intricate. The examples listed above describe the common kinds of striking arrangement.

It is granted at the outset that subtler degrees of distinction exist, that more exact techniques for the analysis of syntax have been developed. But for a number of reasons I have been guided by an analogy with the development of biological science: gross anatomy properly precedes the study of the fine structure of cells. It is true that the "new" grammar, operating on the phonological, phrase structural, and transformational levels, is capable of unprecedented elegance of description and nicety of discrimination. Modern linguists have also made the very provocative suggestion that sentences can be ranked according to "degrees of grammaticalness," and a hierarchy established for the aberrant structures in poetry. There is no doubt that such a grammatical hierarchy would be immensely useful in identifying and distinguishing types of syntactic variation. But we cannot be certain that grammaticality is perfectly coexitensive with some aesthetic quality. It seems highly unlikely, intuitively, that a one-to-one mapping could exist between grammaticalness and poetic effect. We may agree with Edward Stankiewicz that, " by taking into account the underlying linguistic structure, the study of poetic language becomes thus a study of a certain type of rearrangement and modification of the elements of everyday spoken language." [15] But when he goes on to say, "Now, if sequences can in some way be ordered as to the degree of grammaticalness, it may be possible to characterize the language of poetry in terms of the density of these sequences of lower-order grammaticalness," [16] we may observe that "a certain type of rearrangement and modification" has been interpreted as a system potentially highly ordered in a specific way.[17]

At this stage in the development of stylistics, it appears wise to begin by describing certain types of rearrangement and modification in the language of poets, without ranking these variations according to a strictly grammatical principle. The significance of syntactic structures in poetry may be most readily grasped through a comparative study of them. In fact, I adopt as axiomatic M. A. K. Halliday's statement: "Linguistic stylistics is thus essentially a comparative study . . . the more texts are studied, the more said about any one text becomes interesting and relevant." [18] Obviously, to study many texts in great detail is the eventual aim of stylistics; but to begin with, one may profitably concentrate on a few of the most easily and clearly distinguishable traits of style in several writers.

Consequently, this study does not aim primarily at precise stylistic profiles of individual poems or even individual authors; it attempts to chart major shifts in structural patterns common to many poets. Thus, for any given poet, the overall proportion of each syntactic variation to the others is as significant as an occasional, wholly idiosyncratic mannerism. The fact is that many major poets of the 1920s chose regular or fragmentary structures, whereas notable poets 60 years earlier often preferred dislocation and elaboration as variations of the normal pattern. The shift from dislocated-elaborate to regular-fragmentary is indicated by the distribution of figures in the table in Appendix I. Notice that, while both groups employ more fragments than elaborate structures, the number of elaborations—especially multiple elaborations—declines noticeably in the later poets, and this decline is accompanied by a sharp rise in the number of fragments. (Multiple elaborations, incidentally, have been computed in the main entries as single elaborate structures, so the bracketed numbers are additive by the formula $E^{[en]} = E + e\,(n-1)$, if one wishes the total number of elaborations irrespective of sentence boundaries.) The exceptions are interesting: Yeats and Robinson, the only poets in either group to manifest the ED pattern, are closer, chronologically, to the nineteenth century than the others of their group. Also, the greater emphasis on regularity among modern poets is not so much an absolute numerical increase as a proportional one, as for example in William Carlos Williams and Lawrence, where fragments and regular structures overwhelmingly predominate.

In the following two chapters each type of variation has been analyzed individually and in detail; and these chapters have been arranged to correspond to the chronological development in poetic style: dislocation and elaboration, common devices of Victorian poets, are discussed first; fragmentation and regularity last. Each sort of variation has also its own history, which has been, for each, briefly traced. Finally, certain of the four seem to be related in an unexpected fashion; and these interrelations have also been thought worthy of comment.

Exceptions to this facile contrast between Victorian

23

and modern deserve nearly as much attention as the rule itself. In chapter 4 the syntax of two nineteenth-century and two modern poets is examined in order to demonstrate how one may isolate the structuring of language peculiar to individual poets and thereafter relate their stylistic traits to those of earlier or later poets. This detailed study of passages from the work of Hopkins, Yeats, Browning, and Eliot reveals both continuity and change in poetic style between 1870 and 1930. Hopkins' work foreshadows some twentieth-century experiments and also the problem of "obscurity" which these experiments seem to entail, while Yeats introduces another kind of syntactic innovation without abandoning certain habits which he shares with the respectable poets of a previous generation. Similarly Browning is a forerunner of modern poets; and though his style differs markedly from Eliot's in most respects, certain stylistic devices in the latter poet seem to be in part an intensification of tendencies given powerful impetus by Browning's work.

In chapter 5 I have suggested some of the very widest implications of the shift in poetry to fragmentary and regular sentences. In chapter 6, on the other hand, I have attempted to demonstrate how "attention to the syntax of things" may assist the reader to appreciate specific poems. These last chapters, then, make explicit the conclusion to which earlier ones point: syntactic analysis has a legitimate bearing on literary questions, whether they involve a poem, a poet, or a period.

2

Conventional Syntactic Variations

DISLOCATION

AMONG POETS writing in or around 1870, a few enjoyed considerable popularity and prestige or, at least, some notoriety. Five such poets, Bryant, Longfellow, Arnold, Tennyson, and Swinburne, are especially useful in illustrating the kinds of stylistic devices favored by successful poets of this age; and samples of their work receive special attention in this chapter. All of these men can be seen as belonging to a poetic tradition: all employ meter and rhyme; all write often in established genres; none manifests the radical inventiveness of a Hopkins or a Browning. Their similarities provide an opportunity to test the validity of certain syntactic characteristics as coordinates in charting an author's style. An analysis of style in terms of three kinds of deviation from regular sentence patterns is effective if some uniformity is detectable in the samples taken from these five poets and if, at the same time, individual differences are immediately apparent.

With one remarkable exception (Tennyson, whose peculiar modernity is discussed below), all of these poets vary their sentence patterns most often by means of dislocating word groups. Every poem in four samples, a total of 19 complete poems and parts of two others, contained a higher percentage of this deviation than of any other. And of the three main categories of variant structure, dislocation is the only phenomenon to occur in *every* poem in all the five samples. It is thus widespread in and heavily exploited by all these poets.

An easy explanation for this fact immediately suggests itself. Most of these poets cast their material in a rigid rhyme scheme, and all of them adhere more or less to a metrical pattern, so that any device to increase the flexibility of the disposition of words in a line would obviously be of service. That such devices are constantly invoked by most poets writing in the traditional manner is even self-evident. Yet, the startling variety in the degree of dependence on this device of dislocation, among poets equally orthodox in their execution, casts some doubt on any facile correlations. Bryant, for example, maintains a ratio of 29 dislocations to 129 regular sentences without noticeably impairing the flow of his verse; while Longfellow has more dislocations (129) than regular structures (100). For the latter the inverted sentence actually becomes the norm! The exigencies of rhyme and rhythm probably could not justify such heavy reliance on a single device. Furthermore, in the early *Cantos* and in *Hugh Selwyn Mauberley,* Ezra Pound composes some dislocated structures, although he follows no strict rhyme scheme or metrical pattern. Pound's ratio of dislocated to regular structures is, in fact, roughly the same as Bryant's. It appears that dislocation can be a stylistic trait not by any means wholly due to forced compromise with the rigid forms of traditional poetry.

Actually, even in an "uninflected" language like English, the poet finds himself at considerable liberty to alter the order of words in a sentence. And often, not content with the customary ways of varying that order, he takes even more liberties than a generous grammarian would like to allow. As a group, in fact, poets are notoriously disrespectful of the conventions of language, and their irrepressible habit of saying things in an original fashion manifests itself in "ungrammatical" structures, "misplaced" modifiers, or an "impossible" sequence of words. A poet's alterations of normal word order may run to type, and then we can classify him accordingly. Or if many nineteenth-century poets alter order by simply inverting subject and verb, while twentieth-century writers break up a sentence into parts which they then scramble in quite unorthodox combinations—and this difference actually occurs—we have another characteristic distinguishing the poetry of two eras. Thus, although dislocation, as defined in the introduction, may seem the most ill-conceived and incomplete of the categories of syntax upon which this study is based, none of the others provides a clearer distinction between the two literary periods.

A glance at the chart in Appendix I reveals that no variation in the nineteenth century was as common as dislocation. Eight men relied most heavily upon it. Among the twentieth-century poets, only E. E. Cummings varies his sentences primarily by dislocation. Obviously one could not get very far trying to establish a stylistic kinship between Longfellow and Cummings, so that some rudimentary distinction of kinds of dislocation will be necessary for the discussion of individual authors; even so, that dislocation of *any* kind should have become manifestly less popular among poets during this 60-year span is a fact of some significance. For not only did more than half the group of early poets habitually alter the order of their words as a principal means of varying their verse-sentences, but the other half (Bryant is the lone exception) favored this device as their next most common kind of innovation. Thus, for 14 of these 15 nineteenth-century poets, dislocation was one of the two most common of three possible sorts of syntactic variation; while among the later poets it is the least common kind of variation for five poets. Even the extreme numerical proportions of dislocated to regular structures reflect the decline of the popularity of this device. The highest proportion (1.3 to 1) is in Longfellow; the lowest (.1 to 1), in William Carlos Williams. Whether or not we distinguish one kind of dislocation from another, then, we might conclude that this general form of syntactic idiosyncrasy has fallen from favor since 1870 or has been deliberately overlooked by recent poets in favor of other stylistic experiments.

The kinds of dislocation recorded here are limited to rather violent wrenches of major sentence or phrase elements: the verb before the subject, the direct object before the verb, the one-word adjective after the noun, and the adverbial phrase before its verbal-adjective head. Yet in the samples of poetry from around 1870, such dislocation did not ordinarily confuse or obscure meaning. The writer who uses this device most often, Longfellow, relies excessively on "poetic inversion" of subject and verb, noun and adjective, and his verse is unquestionably lucid. Likewise, a line of Lowell, Rossetti, or Morris may have a most contorted structure, a highly "poetic" ring, and at the same time express unequivocally the most banal ideas. Longfellow writes

> Have I dreamed? Or was it real,
>   What I saw as in a vision,
> When to marches hymeneal
>   In the land of the Ideal
> Moved my thought o'er Fields Elysian? [1]

and we record three dislocations, all in one sentence. Like almost all of Longfellow's "variations," these result from *a reversal of the usual sequence of two clearly related grammatical elements.* After the switch, the elements are usually quite as obviously related as they were in their more customary order. Displaced adjectives, for example, are almost never separated from the noun head; they are simply shifted from a position before the noun to one after it, as in "Fields Elysian." Often a morpheme like the s added to singular verb forms in the present tense establishes meaning regardless of word order. Thus, whether we say "So happy feels he" or "He so happy feels," or "He feels so happy," no reader with a good command of English would fail to understand us. Similarly, in the stanza quoted above, all the nouns in the sentence except "thought" hold positions in rigid, conventional phrase structures, so that only "thought" could be the subject of the finite verb. The most salient characteristics of such conventional dislocation are that only some elements in the sentence pattern shift position, and that the shift does not alter or confuse the grammatical relations between such elements. The poet may thus vary the cadence, sound pattern, and emphasis of a line without changing his meaning appreciably.

In certain circumstances, a poet can indeed disjoin radically from their usual sequence a series of grammatical elements. Bryant puts seven words between the two members of a comparative adverb construction:

> Scarce less the cleft-born wild flower seems to enjoy
> Existence, than the winged plunderer
> That sucks its sweets.[2]

But here the phrase "scarce less," itself composed of words in meaningful order, can be shifted as a unit to a position just before "than." Then the word order becomes perfectly normal. Longfellow's broken parallelism is equally easy to mend:

> Pawing the ground they came, and resting their necks on each other,
> And with their nostrils distended inhaling the freshness of evening.[3]

Again, whole coherent sections of the sentence have been placed in unusual positions, but since each section remains integral and continuous, its grammatical function is clear and its position therefore not crucial to the meaning. Adverbs like "usually" or "often," as has been noted, can occur almost anywhere in a sentence. But aside from this peculiar flexibility, the nature of the language seemed to most nineteenth-century poets to restrict syntactic manipulation to only those shifts of major sentence units which preserved (1) the definite grammatic significance of these units in relation to one another and (2) the order of words within the larger units.

A quite different sort of dislocation is that of interruption, which classical rhetoricians called the *parenthesis*. Here the natural order of words in a sentence does not change but merely fractures to admit extraneous words which are generally syntactically irrelevant to the separated members of the fractured sentence. The typographical marks called "parentheses" are incidentally not the only indication of such interruption; the dash serves oftener as a sign of it.

An interruption produces in a reader effects very different from those of ordinary dislocation. In the first place, one may not always simply rearrange the interrupted parts to reconstruct a single, coherent, grammatical sentence, identical in meaning to the dislocated version. The interruption, though unorthodox, may impose a rigid logic of its own on the sentence; then the intruding elements can function correctly only if they intrude *where* they do. Examples of this tight but ungrammatical bond between interruptor and framing sentence appear throughout the work of Browning, a recognized master of this technique.

>   . . . I found this book,
>   Gave a lira for it, eightpence English just,

30

(Mark the predestination!) when a Hand,
Always above my shoulder, pushed me once . . .[4]

. . . In due time like reply
Came from the so-styled Patron of the Poor,
Official mouthpiece of the five accused
Too poor to fee a better,—Guido's luck
Or else his fellows',—which, I hardly know,—
An outbreak as of wonder at the world,
A fury-fit of outraged innocence,
A passion of betrayed simplicity . . .[5]

. . . 'Twas the so-styled Fisc began,
Pleaded (and since he only spoke in print
The printed voice of him lives now as then)
The public prosecutor—"Murder's proved . . ."[6]

I learn this from epistles which begin
Here where the print ends,—see the pen and ink
Of the advocate, the ready at a pinch!—
"My client . . ."[7]

In only one case is the interrupting sentence obviously bound to its context: the pronouns in the third
selection make sense only when they occur near the
antecedent "Fisc." Elsewhere, the bridges are semantic,
not grammatical. The fragment "Guido's luck . . ."
would mean nothing disjoined from the sentence in
which it is buried. But uttered as a cryptic comment on
Guido's poverty and the dubious value of his legal
counsel, it can occur only after "too poor to fee a
better." This reading of the phrase becomes less likely,
or even very unlikely, if the phrase is shifted to some
other point within the sentence.

The last two quotations illustrate well enough the
virtue of this kind of dislocation for dramatic monologue, wherein an author tries to convey the immediacy

and spontaneity of speech. Browning manages to conjure his material from past to present, printed page to living drama, by inserting a sentence with a shift in tense ("and since he *spoke* in print, the printed voice of him *lives* now as then") between the verb "pleaded" —note past form—and the subject "public prosecutor" of the sentence which introduces the very text of the plea. In the very act of stating what *was* said, the poet decides to think of it as *being* said. Similarly, in the last passage quoted, Browning communicates the illusion of an immediate reading of his old yellow book by admonishing his "audience," after the phrase "here where the print ends," to notice the contrast of pen and ink scrawl to typeset lettering. The exhortation seems designed only to create this illusion of an actual sequence of mental events and could thus occur no where else in the sentence. A peruser of the manuscript could doubtless finish the printed part, note the shift to handwriting and reflect for an instant on the resourceful perseverance of a lawyer's keeping of records, and then pick up the thread of his reading.

Dislocation by interruption may profoundly alter the cadence and momentum of the verse line, but unlike the traditional reshuffling of elements in one sentence, this alteration makes the structure of poetry imitate the structure of ordinary speech—or even the less coherent pattern of unspoken but verbalized thought. "Poetic inversion" marks a style as mannered, artificial, for the most part unlike all other discourse in the language; but the device of interrupting the normal word order of one sentence by another sentence or by a fragment gives poetry one of the most obvious characteristics of common, unpremeditated, colloquial language.[8]

Poets after Browning relied heavily on this device; and although no consistent record of the proportion of traditional dislocations to interruptions was kept, the rapid decline in popularity of the former was almost certainly matched by an increased predilection for the latter. Four of Sandburg's seven dislocations, three of Williams' nine, twenty-five of Cummings' sixty-nine were interruptions. Such proportions did not occur in samples from the earlier poets, Browning excepted. Thus, both the waning of the artificial variety of dislocation and the heightened vigor of the colloquial sort help distinguish modern poetry from its antecedents.

There are other distinctions to be drawn. Ordinary Longfellowesque inversion does not alter the significance of a sentence; nor do interruptions ordinarily confuse or destroy the grammatical links binding words into a sentence, however much its meaning may be altered by the invisible semantic "radiations" of the material. Some twentieth-century poets, however, indulge in disarrangements that defy one's attempts to find ordinary structures of equivalent meaning.

D. H. Lawrence's "Tortoise Shout" contains the following lines, punctuated as a discrete structure:

A far was-it-audible scream,
Or did it sound on the plasm direct? [9]

The reader could not fail to recognize that the two questions are logically but not grammatically parallel; and that to meddle with this asymmetry (writing "A far scream—was it audible, or did it . . . ?") would alter the effect of the lines, for immediately registering "a far scream" really forestalls doubt of its audibility. Turning the first question into an adjective before a noun renders identification of the impulse hesitant and uncertain. Lawrence achieves fidelity to the pattern of sensation and tentative response, at the expense of grammatical orthodoxy.

But none of the poets in this study disrupts and disorders his sentences as radically as E. E. Cummings. His odd structures range from an unusual number of interruptions,

> let (however) us
> Walk very (therefore and) softly among one's own
> memory (but) along perhaps the
> By invisibilities
>   spattered (or if
> it may be socalled) memory
> Of (without more ado about less
> than nothing
>   2 boston
> Dolls. . . .[10]

to highly idiosyncratic dislocations of major sentence
elements,

> (he, slightly whom or
> cautiously this person
> and this imitation resemble,
> descends into the earth with the year
> a cigarette between his ghost-lips
> gradually [11]

even more idiosyncratic dislocation of words within
the major elements,

> . . . (but if i
> should say
> Now the all saucers
> but cups if begin to spoons dance every-
> should where say over the damned table and we
> hold lips Eyes everything
> hands you know what
> happens). . . .[12]

and, finally, the scrambling of parts of words, mor-
phemes, or even phonemes.

> helves surling out of eakspeasies per (reel) hap-
>   singly

proregress heandshe-ingly people
trickle curselaughgroping shrieks bubble
squirmwrither staggerful unstrolls collaps ingly
flash a of-faceness stuck thumblike into pie
is traffic this recalls hat gestures bud
plumbtumbling hand voices Eye Doangivuh suddenly immense impotently Eye Doancare Eye
And How replies the upsquirtingly careens
the to collide flatfooting with Wushyuname
a girl-flops to the Geddup curb leans
carefully spewing into her own Shush Shame
as (out from behind Nowhere) creeps the deep
    thing
everybody sometimes calls morning.[13]

The third passage can, indeed, be reconstructed as a
grammatical statement: (but if I should say Now, but
if we should say everything, hold hands, lips and Eyes,
you know what happens—all the cups, saucers, spoons
begin to dance everywhere over the damned table).
But certain words ("everywhere," "and," "everything")
and the phrase "over the damned table" could as well
be shifted to other positions, with slight changes in
meaning. In the last selection, although some feasible
structures can be formulated by transposing parts of
words and phrases into new patterns, there is no cer-
tainty that any one of these patterns is "equivalent"
to the original. Here, certainly, the grammatical links
between words—or even parts of words—have been
so confused or obliterated that no certain reconstruction of normal sentence patterns is possible. One must
consider such poetry as possessing its own unique grammar or as containing a number of simultaneously possible recombinations of its elements.

Often, no matter how he composes the pieces of the
puzzle, the reader finds himself left with a few fragments. Indeed, one has perfectly legitimate grounds
for describing these last selections as fragmentary. The

sentence framework has been utterly shattered, and the reader simply makes up his own patterns from the debris. To provide such passages with some sort of grammatical coherence, he must relate words simply because they occur on the same page together and in the same poem. According to the definitions devised for this study, only the "leftovers" which cannot be fitted into such tentative reconstructions have been identified as fragments; but it is easy to see that radical dislocation can give to poetry an appearance and impact like those which fragmentary styles have. This resemblance is particularly strong when the syntax is so disturbed that a reader is deprived of even the most elementary conventional signs identifying the functions of words.

Then dislocation and fragmentation seem indistinguishable, as in the last quotation, where several words can function equally well—but not jointly—in the same role in a hypothetical "sentence," or one word can have more than one role in several sentences. Thus, for example, the words "trickle," "flash," "gestures" can be either nouns or verbs, and "this" could act as subject for either "is" or "recalls" (but not both). In any event the choice of a particular word for a unique role may immediately make fragments of the alternative candidates for the position. There is, after all, no indication that the poet would condone even these tentative attempts to superimpose on his style a quasi-orthodox syntax, and every reason to suspect that he intends not only to use adverbs or verbs as if they were adjectives or nouns but also to leave quite undetermined or ambiguous the essential grammatical function of large blocs of words.

Obviously, this sort of dislocation differs fundamentally from the dislocations of Longfellow and Browning. Cummings' shifts involve more than the major constituents of a sentence taken as units. He appears deliberately to addle grammatical signals and sense

36

(heandshe-ingly, unstrolls), or to make the order of words irrelevant to their function (the upsquirtingly careens the to collide). In short, he sometimes destroys conventional syntactic relations and offers the reader mere fragments or, perhaps, a new syntax and new vocabulary. Colloquial locutions are certainly not the model for such alterations. Unlike Hopkins, the only other poet of the 30 who also experiments daringly with word order, Cummings does not often attempt to render the rhythm of impassioned speech. It is also doubtful that concern for metrical patterns could lead to such innovations. Music may enhance but ought not to drown out sense. Does he seek, then, a perverse variety for its own sake, seemingly at any cost? For the moment this question must be unanswered, since it involves the whole problem of the aims and methods of a certain kind of modern verse; but the later discussion of the fragment poses like questions, and at that point the *raison d'être* for such radicalism will be explored.

ELABORATION

IN RATHER OBVIOUS and sharp contrast to poets like Eliot, Pound, or Frost, the group of five famous earlier poets (Tennyson, Arnold, Swinburne, Longfellow, and Bryant) also relies often on elaboration as a means of achieving variety, contrast, or other more specific effects. Like dislocation, elaboration can increase the range and flexibility of poetic language without shattering the framework of conventional grammar. Generally, elaboration seems to occur among these poets more consistently than the more radical and agrammatical trait of fragmentation. The opposite is true, according to the table in Appendix I, of most of the modern writers whose styles have been examined. In all the poems selected from Bryant and Swinburne, elabora-

37

tion is a more common phenomenon than fragmentation; and though this predominance persists in only half the sample poems of both Longfellow and Arnold, elaboration is still for these five poets the more consistent variation: only one poem from all the samples taken together lacks it entirely, while five contain no fragments at all. A poet like Pound, on the other hand, in a space of 500 lines writes 207 fragments and only five elaborate "structures"—three of which are elaborate *fragments!*

The degree and kind of elaboration employed by these nineteenth-century writers varies greatly, so that, again, differences are readily distinguishable between individuals sharing a common tedency. At one extreme, Tennyson has elaborated only 11 sentences in a text containing 268 regular ones. Swinburne, at the other extreme, has 43 elaborations out of 88 regular sentences. And of these 43, seven are double and one is a triple elaboration; that is, some of Swinburne's sentences contain ten finite verbs, or two series of four grammatically parallel elements, or a combination of at least five verbs and one or more series of modifiers. It is interesting to note that all of these poets, including Tennyson, furnished at least one example of double elaboration, while such doubling occurs more rarely in the group of samples taken from a later generation.

A writer elaborates in order to gain range in the pace and scope of a poem; and in some of the samples it is possible to find refinements on this technique which seem responsible for certain specific effects on the reader. These refinements, and the effects they provoke, have ultimately a relation to a subsequent discussion of certain structures found in more recent poetry. This relation justifies dwelling briefly on a few examples in order to make precise certain aspects of elaboration.

One ancestor of the elaborate construction, as the following passage from Bryant's poem "The Song of the Sower" seems to indicate, may be the epic simile.

Bryant disguises a rather sudden and violent shift in subject and in tone by means of an implied metaphor and a simple, overt, but very extended comparison. This extension, in fact, succeeds in shifting completely the reader's focus of attention and his mood; what seems at first a radical digression is thus achieved smoothly, continuously.

Ha! feel ye not your fingers thrill,
    As o'er them, in the yellow grains,
Glide the warm drops of blood that fill,
    For Mortal strife, the warrior's veins;
Such as, on Solferino's day,
Slaked the brown sand and flowed away;—
Flowed till the herds, on Mincio's brink
Snuffed the red stream and feared to drink;—
Blood that in deeper pools shall lie,
    On the sad earth, as time grows gray,
When men by deadlier arts shall die,
    And deeper darkness blot the sky
    Above the thundering fray. . . .[14]

Besides the elaboration of new subject matter, this single structure enlarges the scope of the poem by unifying images from the past, present, and future into a single, sustained vision. The significant images, however, appear to be those contained in the long subordinate elements, which are attached to a rather weak rhetorical question acting as the "main clause" in a grammarian's terminology. This peculiar imbalance allows the poet to introduce a quite new topic and develop it at some length, without apparently dropping an earlier subject which still receives a purely structural emphasis. Epic similes function in this way. Here, however, Bryant elaborates a sentence in order to manage a thematic development. The comparison is not really a digression, but an extended counterpoint, offsetting the image of pouring yellow grain, symbol of life and growth, with others of bloodshed and darkness.

This elaborate structure also develops in an interesting fashion. After the comparison is begun, the series of clauses within clauses—a kind of development we might call the "Chinese box" method—is made to cohere tightly by means of the repetition of certain words or of certain key concepts. The verb "flowed" occurs twice, almost in immediate sequence, and its second appearance introduces the long subordinate clause hinging on the conjunction "till." It is worth noting that this second verb, set off from its twin by dashes, resembles a fragment, since it not only merely replicates a preceding verb but also appears sharply disjoined from the subject of that verb. Still, the repetition serves to bind one clause unambiguously and grammatically to another. The whole chain of clauses is related to the main clause by the semantic overlap of "glide" and "flow," the verbs which inaugurate and sustain the metaphor.

The most important linking device here, however, is probably the pair of structures built on the repeated noun "blood." The phrase "warm drops of blood" and the single noun "blood" hold crucial positions: from each depends a relative clause which adds a whole dimension to the new theme stated explosively by the word "blood" itself, and the parallelism of the clauses reinforces the simple link provided by the repetition of the word. Later, in a discussion of the fragment, it will be instructive to recall this incident of the single noun as a node powerful enough to organize and develop complex thought around itself.

These characteristics of elaboration are not peculiar to Bryant; they appear much more prominently in Swinburne, whose predeliction for this device is not fairly represented by statistics, striking as these latter are. If this poet's double and triple elaborations were counted as groups of single ones, the totals would show a ratio of about two elaborations for every three regular structures. But since an elaboration is by definition an inordinately long and complicated sentence, a Swinburne poem would generally consist largely of elaborated passages; that is, most of the lines—stanzas—in it would be part of some elaborate structure. The point may be partly grasped by noting that Swinburne alone of this group of writers furnished fewer than 100 regular sentences over a space of 700 lines of poetry, and that he composed at least twice and usually three times as many elaborate structures as any of the others.

A Swinburnian double elaboration from "The Ballad of Death" will suffice to illustrate the effect of this extraordinary exploitation of one kind of syntax.

> Upon her raiment of dyed sendaline
> Were painted all the secret ways of love
> And covered things thereof,
> That hold delight as grape-flowers hold their
>   wine;
> Red mouths of maidens and red feet of doves,
> And brides that kept within the bride-chamber
> Their garment of soft shame,
> And weeping faces of the wearied loves
> That swoon in sleep and awake warier,
> With heat of lips and hair shed out like flame.[15]

Again, repetition of words or concepts helps bind the parts of the structure together: "dyed," "painted," "wine," "red mouths," "red feet," form one series; "maidens," "brides," "faces" perhaps another. The series of "that" clauses depending from three of these nouns reinforces the linking. Alliteration, of course, binds parts of individual lines together. The method of proliferation seen here acts much like that in the Bryant sentence, although the two examples are structurally different. In both a series of nouns becomes a group of kernels which can sprout extended new structures.

Perhaps to prevent the reader from getting lost in these new growths, the kernel nouns have semantic similarities or, sometimes, are identical.

In this particular passage, the "main clause" consists of a weak passive verb, its locative complement, and the generalized subjects "secret ways of love" and "covered things," which the string of appositive noun phrases in effect replaces. As in Bryant's extended simile, an imbalance occurs because the specific, concrete images, as well as the notable *activities* in the sentence (keeping within, swooning, waking), are concentrated in structures generated by the series of nouns—itself depending from the generalized subjects. Refining within the frame of a relatively weak and vague assertion, the poet creates detailed, vivid portraits. The energy of the verbs is thus not transmitted from sentence to sentence with cumulative intensity, as in narration or argument, but is diffused within a closed system; the structure is not dynamic, but static. What forceful statements there are depart as radii from an unmoving point—the noun kernel.

This pattern, a weak statement (usually passive) from which radiate intricate dependent clauses "hinged" on important nouns, may in part account for the tone of some of Swinburne's verse. The languor, the sensation of exhausted passion, the portrait-like quality of many poems—these have a parallel in the complex replications and extensions of a peculiar sentence pattern. The heavy brocade of imagery becomes more intrinsically interesting than the flounce or swirl of the fabric —and, thus, of more concern than the wearer of the gown, be she Faustine, Venus, or Proserpine. But of course these ladies may be thought of as the key nouns from which entire poems are ultimately generated. In such a view, the noun would be the central, dominant element in a certain style of poetry.

Before exploring this possibility, one might point out examples of this kind of noun- (or pronoun-) generated elaboration in other poets. For example, the device of repetition in "Rugby Chapel" borders on becoming an unpleasant mannerism, like stuttering.

> We, we have chosen our path,—
> Path to a clear-purposed goal,
> Path of advance. . . .
> . . . .
> We were weary, and we
> Fearful, and we in our march
> Fain to drop down and to die.[16]

One of the starkest illustrations of this phenomenon occurs in Tennyson ("The Defense of Lucknow"):

> . . . and there hail'd on our houses and halls
> Death from their rifle-bullets, and death from their
> cannon-balls,
> Death in our innermost chamber, and death at our
> slightest barricade,
> Death while we stood with the musket, and death
> while we stoopt to the spade,
> Death to the dying, and wounds to the wounded,
> for often there fell
> Striking the hospital wall, crashing thro' it, their
> shot and their shell,
> Death—for their spies were among us, their marksmen were told of our best . . .[17]

This elaborate structure and the group of sentences which follows it develop internal, cohesive bonds rather different from those noted in earlier examples. In company with one or two further passages drawn from Swinburne, this quotation allows us to perceive some continuity between Victorian and modern poetry.

At first the long string of identical nouns ("death") with their accompanying modifiers appears to be a rather obvious method of elaboration: All the nouns,

43

in perfect parallelism, act as a compound subject. But this rigid, grammatical structure is in part illusory, for the sense of the passage, and of what follows it, does not accord well with such a reading. If each of the *death*s shared equal value as a subject of the verb "hailed," then one would have to try to make sense out of such sentences as "there hail'd on our houses and halls . . . Death in our innermost chamber . . . and death while we stoopt to the spade." Can a barrage hail simultaneously on and *in* a building? And does one use a spade indoors—else why should the diggers be mortally concerned about the bombardment of house and hall? Further, does not the one variant subject "wounds to the wounded" go lamely enough with the verb "hailed?"

It seems likely, in fact, that beginning with the third "subject" in the series ("Death in our innermost chamber") the association of the repeated nouns to the preceding verb grows faint. The nouns begin to take on autonomous force, and from a compressed metaphor meaning "cannonballs" the word "death" shifts to its ordinary function as an abstract noun. Realizing, apparently, that he has been derailed from his original metaphor, the poet suddenly returns to it and makes it explicit. Focusing on the specific case of the hospital, he fashions a second sentence on the model of the first, but replaces the word "death" with its earlier literal equivalent, "their shot and their shell." Then occurs a very interesting locution: Tennyson repeats the key noun "death" for the eighth and last time, apparently as a very loose appositive phrase equivalent to "their shot and their shell," reintroducing, in effect, the metaphor. The effect of this oscillation is to bind together in a unique fashion the two sentences of like model: the final "death" obviously relates the second sentence to the first thematically, yet it simultaneously exerts a powerful attraction on the two preceding noun phrases "death to the dying, and wounds to the wounded," which obviously depend for their significance on the second and more specific assertion. Thus, the abrupt reintroduction of the metaphor generates a sort of "backlash" structure, in which the last "death" is in apposition to the second subject and collects around itself the two earlier noun phrases as dislocated modifiers, depriving them, in other words, of much of their value as compound subjects of the first verb "hail'd."

For two reasons, then, this passage may be said to illustrate the manner in which fragmentation could develop out of excessive elaboration. First, the early metaphorical force of the key noun disintegrates, though this change has no structural earmarks, and subsequent uses of this noun in a nominally parallel series establish for it an autonomous value; the last items in the series seem only faintly and uncertainly connected to the original sentence. Then, the key noun occurs last in a second sentence, into whose structure it fits only with a severe semantic wrench; and in this last appearance it draws with it—into a partial or shared orbit, so to speak—those nouns whose relation to a previous structure has grown weak or ambiguous. It appears that unless a reader is willing to deny the probable sense of the passage, he must ignore some conventional structural links and view this string of nouns not as simple elaboration, but as a series interrupted by some autonomous, some "hovering" elements which possess, at least in part, the character of fragments.

Somewhat similar problems arise in connection with certain lines in Swinburne, and again the elaboration of a string of nouns seems to allow a degree of ambiguity, of conflict between the significance of a word group considered independently and its meaning within the structure of a sentence.

O Love's lute heard about the lands of death,
Left hanged upon the trees that were therein;
O Love and Time and Sin,

Three singing mouths that mourn now under-
    breath,
Three lovers, each one evil spoken of;
O smitten lips wherethrough this voice of mine
Came softer with her praise;
Abide a little for our lady's love.[18]

In this series of noun phrases (finally marked an elaboration after much deliberation), the potential relations
between the individual elements of the series can be
reduced to definite alternatives insofar as one seeks
only grammatical coherence. The series consists of
either six exclamatory fragments followed by one noun
phrase used as a vocative with the verb "abide," or
seven noun phrases in apposition, used collectively as
vocatives with the same verb. The pattern of repetitions and the semantic linking of key nouns suggest
however, relations not immediately compatible with
the grammatical ones. Besides the lack of exclamation
points which would clearly mark the boundaries of
ordinary fragments, the series of nouns has a number
of semantic links. It would be difficult to ignore the
similarities between "smitten lips" and the silent lute,
and "mouths that mourn now underbreath," to say
nothing of the repetition of "love." At the same time,
giving equal force and grammatical status to all the
phrases would lead to some strange figures. Consider
the sense of the passage so interpreted: "O Love's
lute . . . O Love . . . and Time and Sin . . . three
lovers . . . Abide a little for our lady's love." Here the
key noun "love" does not seem to be repeated in order
to reinforce a grammatical pattern; in fact it appears
to confuse that pattern. Reading "O Love . . . abide a
little for our lady's love" introduces a puzzling play on
a word.

Finally, the most clearly equated elements in the
noun series, the three lines beginning with "O Love
and Time and Sin" and ending with the semicolon form

46

a group of five nouns or noun phrases with semantic links to the preceding and following noun phrases (Love's lute—Love and three lovers; mouths—lips and voice) so that the whole series is to a degree coherent and expressive by itself. The implied metaphor relating Love's lute, the mourning lover's lips, and the "singing mouths" of Love, Time and Sin gives a semblance of thematic unity to the series of nouns. Tenuous enough to begin with, this unity disintegrates entirely when the author attempts to fit the whole hazy metaphor into a traditional sentence pattern; when in short he compels the nouns to function in a sentence, to act or be acted upon, or, to put it another way, when he declines to allow them their own integrity.

In this selection, then, as in the three earlier examples of elaboration, a poet creates patterns based on the partial autonomy of a group of nouns or noun phrases which themselves form an expressive unit. Bryant's sentence, probably the most "correct" and least controversial of the selections, employs relative clauses to expand a single image into a thematic variation within his poem. This expansion creates imbalance between the apparent main clause, or assertion, and the extended elaborations built around some of its constituent nouns. Tennyson, in the structure quoted above, departs from stringent grammar and makes of repetition an organizing principle which replaces or overrides traditional grammatical relations. As Tennyson exploits it, this technique binds elements only very loosely, allowing to them a greater degree of independence and allowing, too, the possibility of ambiguities. The first selection from Swinburne maintains grammatical integrity, but the imbalance between the assertion and its accompanying elaborations seems much greater than in the Bryant passage. This imbalance grows to an uncomfortable tension in the second Swinburne example, where the true "center of meaning" seems to occur in the group of nouns with their implied metaphorical links, not in the feeble and anticlimactic assertion to which the group is grammatically appended. But in all these cases it is clear that elaboration, if it is extensive enough, can encourage a certain autonomy and organizing power of the noun at the expense of diminished emphasis on the dynamic element of a sentence, its verb.

This conclusion has an obvious bearing on the study of fragments. Aside from occasional abbreviated clauses, colloquial omissions of subjects, and elliptical responses to questions, the fragments recorded in this study consist of nouns or noun phrases which may generate extensive dependent structures. And while a conventional sentence, without sacrificing grammatical coherence, can be elaborated by means of the repetition of key nouns or key concepts; a noun, acting independently, may originate a pattern depending almost solely on these semantic rather than grammatical relations. Thus the noun is the irreducible, primary element of fragments, elaborate or simple, much as the verb is central in the ordinary sentence; and fragments can be linked by the repetition of key words, as sentences are related by means of grammatical signals (pronouns, conjunctive adverbs, parallel structure, and the like).

Fragments containing a noun as primary element occur widely in the poetry of Whitman, Pound, and Eliot; but Tennyson also—surprisingly enough—relied heavily on this structure in his later work. He does not often weld a series of fragments into a larger pattern, as Pound does, but he provides good examples of the rudimentary function of this device. And in a passage like that given above, one glimpses the potential of repetition and semantic overlap as a way of integrating fragments or quasi-fragments into a larger, more intricate pattern.

Tennyson also furnishes examples of less common kinds of fragments. There is a dislocated fragment in "Locksley Hall Sixty Years After":

> . . . iron hearted victors they.[19]

This structure derives from the most common form of fragmentation, in which a copula has apparently been dropped and two or more nouns simply juxtaposed. Usually this form is technically indistinguishable from two fragments with a strong, obvious semantic link (synonymity), but here the noun and pronoun are bound by a supplementary grammatical link (the plural *s* and the person and number of the pronoun), so that a single verbless fragment is formed. In the same poem occurs another interesting series of fragments:

> there . . .
> Lies my Amy dead in childbirth, dead the mother,
> dead the child.[20]

The two noun phrases, "dead the mother" and "dead the child," are obviously related to the preceding sentence by means of repeated words, yet they have no apparent grammatical function in that sentence and must be counted fragments. But here, too, the reader may feel that copulas are missing, and that he could reconstruct a sentence: "Dead (is) the mother, dead (is) the child." Possibly because the phrases and the preceding sentence are both inverted, though differently (The mother (is) dead, Dead (is) the mother; My Amy lies there dead, There lies my Amy dead), these two fragments have an illusory orthodoxy; they seem to act as eliptical parallel clauses. Certainly, the sense of the passage is clear.

In the above examples a reader tends to reconstruct a grammatical statement around the fragment. He is like an archaeologist who finds the largest shard and can easily reconstruct the shape and dimensions of a whole pot. But Tennyson has at times attempted to intrigue the reader with less simple reconstructions.

49

neously experimenting as radically with syntactic forms as any modern has yet done. It is nevertheless interesting that some points of continuity exist between poets as typical of their times as Tennyson and Pound. Such continuity, if it can be demonstrated, would immediately suggest some possible modifications of the usual view of the twentieth-century revolt against Victorian mannerisms. All questions of diction and subject matter aside, it would appear that poets of and after Pound's generation have not broken sharply with the style of their predecessors, but have exaggerated certain syntactic idiosyncrasies already partially developed. The originality of the later poets lies in their attempt to make these idiosyncracies into not variant but *standard* structures—structures capable of forming a meaningful pattern as large as a whole poem.

In Bryant's extended simile, in Swinburne's excessively diffuse repletions, and in Tennyson's inordinately loose and sometimes ambiguous modifiers, there emerge certain unusual syntactic characteristics with a common base. These poets extend or modify a poetic theme by generating from one noun or a group of nouns complex, dependent structures. The dependent structures often are related to the noun kernel by means of clear, traditional grammatical signals; but this primary noun may itself have only an implicit or uncertain relation to its context (usually a sentence, surrounding or adjoining it), or it may generate a passage whose importance is out of keeping with the grammatical emphasis the noun receives in its context. Consequently, the noun and its subordinate elements tend to become to a degree autonomous. To forge links between these partially independent units, the nineteenth-century poet may rely on repeating the noun but altering its modification, or on implicit semantic bonds between juxtaposed nouns, or on supplementary grammatical signals from which a sentence (usually with copulative verb) may be reconstructed. Thus, the development of the independent noun phrase and of unorthodox methods of connecting such phrases can be traced in part, at least, to the unusually elaborate sentences of late Victorian writers.

3

A New Manner

PIECING OUT WITH THE IMAGINATION

IT HAS ALREADY been suggested that a fragmentary style gives primary emphasis to the noun, and that the great majority of fragments are classified as such because they contain a noun or noun phrase which lacks a finite verb to provide grammatical "sense" to the structure. Excessive elaboration, then—especially in the form of a string of noun phrases—may form an intermediary stage between narrative verse of strict grammatical orthodoxy and the highly fragmented poetry of some twentieth-century writers. But what of the techniques of relating grammatically autonomous nouns? Does the style of Tennyson in this respect have anything in common with that of Pound, whose first few *Cantos* contain far more fragments than regular sentences?

Any poet attempting, so to speak, to write sentences without main verbs faces the same problem: How does one get from noun to noun; that is, how can a bridge of meaning be established between nouns whose only apparent relation is that they appear on the same page together? Further, can a poet hope to formulate patterns of some variety and subtlety out of such material? It is not surprising that those trying to find solutions to these problems have developed similar stylistic traits. Pound and Tennyson, in fact, have resorted

54

to similar devices as a means of exploiting the special effects of which the fragment is capable.

Given the results of the tabulation of lines from Pound, one readily expects to find in this poet the most obvious examples of the use of these devices. In the five hundred lines taken from Cantos II, III, and IV and from *Hugh Selwyn Mauberley*, there were 207 fragments and only 133 regular structures. Of elaborations there were only five—and three of these were elaborate fragments (an interesting parallel with Tennyson, who also composed elaborate fragments). The nineteenth-century poets, it has been remarked, consistently wrote traditional fragments in the form of exclamations or colloquial elliptical phrases. Of Pound's more than two hundred fragmentary structures only four could be clearly considered of this variety. Also, in Cantos II and IV, fragments outnumber regular structures in a ratio of more than two to one. Obviously, Pound has attempted what none of his five famous predecessors dared, the construction of poems (or large, unified sections of poems) primarily out of fragments.

The device of linking fragments by repeating key words, especially nouns, appears throughout passages from Pound. The multiplicity of these repetitions and their combination with other techniques—supplementary grammatical signals like pronouns, semantic connections, and implied parallelism—can shape patterns of a length and complexity far exceeding anything heretofore examined.

> Actaeon . . .
>   and a valley
> The valley is thick with leaves, with leaves, the
>   trees,
> The sunlight glitters, glitters a-top,
> Like a fish-scale roof,
>   Like the church roof in Poictiers
> If it were gold.

Beneath it, beneath it
Not a ray, not a slivver, not a spare disc of sunlight
Flaking the black, soft water;
Bathing the body of nymphs, of nymphs, and
    Diana,
Nymphs, white-gathered about her, and the air,
    air,
Shaking, air alight with the goddess, fanning their
    hair in the dark,
Lifting, lifting and wafting:
Ivory dipping in silver,
    Shadow'd, o'ershadow'd
Ivory dipping in silver,
Not a splotch, not a lost shatter of sunlight.
Then Actaeon: Vidal,
Vidal. It is old Vidal speaking, stumbling along in
    the wood,
Not a patch, not a lost shimmer of sunlight, the
    pale hair of the goddess.[1]

A few of the fragments in this passage are linked by grammatical signals; namely, the pronouns "her" and "their." A few others are bound—mechanically enough —by the strong parallelism of the "not" + (noun) construction. It is also true that the quotation begins and ends with at least partially grammatical sentences. But by and large this whole passage is held together by means of repeated key nouns: "Actaeon," "sunlight," "nymphs," "goddess," "ivory," "hair." Besides their repetition, these nouns relate to others through an intricate chain of semantic overlapping. Thus, nymphs "white-gathered" relate to ivory; and the bathing of the nymphs is then expressed metaphorically, for silver, through the implications of the participle "dipping," is identified with water; and in turn the phrase "black, soft water"— in company with the adverbial modifier "beneath it" where "it" refers to "roof" and thus to the canopy of leaves—associates the shaded pool with the important phrases on the model "not + (noun) of sunlight," and the key noun "sunlight" of course is related by the verb "glitters a-top" to the tree-roof and therefore to the valley "thick with leaves"—and therefore also to Actaeon. Again the unlucky mortal, the secret pool, the fair goddess—but surely the ingredients of the old legend are being combined in a new way.

The manner in which the two or three "sentences" melt into a series of fragments deserves some comment. "The valley is thick with leaves" and "It is old Vidal speaking" are both assertions of that static, descriptive sort already observed in some of the "main" clauses in Swinburne; the unattached phrases "a valley thick with leaves" and "old Vidal speaking" carry almost as much force as the sentences with neutral copulatives. And indeed, Pound seems to abandon any pretense of orthodox grammatical coherence even before he terminates these sentences clearly. From the adverbial phrase "with leaves" he shifts abruptly over a comma to the autonomous noun "trees" and then begins either another sentence or a clause ("The sunlight glitters . . .") without any grammatical signal connecting it to the preceding sentence. The link between "leaves" and "trees" is obviously semantic and not in any way grammatical. It might be added that the reader must wholly disallow ordinary grammar a few lines further, for the phrase "beneath it" can only make sense if one makes the pronoun refer to "roof" and deduces that this word must be a figure for "trees" since the sun can "glitter a-top" both. Ordinarily, however, this pronoun would refer specifically to the immediately preceding one, which itself stands for the church roof in Poictiers. Finally, one must refuse a reading of the last sentence which would make of "wood," "patch," "shimmer" and "pale hair" nouns in apposition. The last three must therefore be fragments juxtaposed in some nongrammatical pattern and grafted directly onto a sentence.

57

The whole passage demands from a reader the recognition and acceptance of a new way of reading poetry. He must grasp the principle of allowing nouns and the extensive substructures they generate to replace sentences, and he must be willing to experiment with unorthodox ways of relating these blocks of nouns. Then the poets aim becomes a bit clearer. By means of participles, "flaking," "bathing," "fanning," "dipping," Pound portrays a series of continuous and simultaneous actions without the sense of separation, restriction—even of *finality*—that a finite verb with its defined tense, mood, and person usually conveys. Therefore, these actions do not advance in a narrative sequence and are thus subordinate to the noun images to which they are attached. The result is a highly visual tableau made up largely of dark and light areas: the trees in bright sun, beneath them the dark pool, the white bodies of nymphs visible in the diffused radiance of the goddess's pale hair. The total effect is not unlike that of an impressionist painting where bright, contrasting colors and indistinct outline create the illusion of glancing, vibrating light and thus of instantaneous movement. Consequently, "old Vidal stumbling along in the wood," the phrase acting as a bridge between a sentence and a sequence of fragments, fits spatially, not grammatically, into the pattern of the images through the association of "wood" to the forest scene already alive in the reader's mind, where a leaf canopy shuts out sunlight and pale hair glimmers in the shade.

Most of the fragments in the selections from Pound fit into larger patterns. These patterns are not often as intricate as the one just examined, but even the few links unifying a briefer passage may produce subtle and unusual effects.

> And by the curved, carved foot of the couch,
>   claw-foot and lion head, an old man seated
> Speaking in the low drone. . . .[2]

The arrangement of these noun phrases illustrates some of the flexibility of which the fragment is capable. All the words except the pair of nouns "claw-foot and lion head" can be subordinated grammatically to one kernel noun "old man." And at first the repetition of the word "foot" and the alliteration of "curved," "carved," and "claw" seem evidence enough to warrant reading the pair as an appositional descriptive phrase displaced from normal position before "of the couch." Yet, as in the excerpt from Tennyson in which a fragment interrupted a more or less normal sequence of words and rendered its sense ambiguous, this displacement gives the two nouns a degree of liberty to form other relations. As a result, a feeble semantic link between "lion head" and "old man" may be slightly emphasized. Repeated encounters with figures patched up out of two nouns, like "claw-foot" and "lion head," characteristic of a fragmentary style, encourage such free and easy rapprochement; and whatever nuances a fragment may possess usually derive from this kind of deliberately indeterminate relation to a context.

Oddly enough, in the light of later accusations of obscurity and difficulty leveled at Pound, this poet ostensibly claimed to favor a return to the phrasing of common speech; for him, the tendencies toward simple, colloquial sentence structure and toward fragmentation were not divergent but really one and the same thing. And it is amusing to note that he thought of Tennyson as the antithesis of this kind of poetry.

> About your "La Flor": it is good. It is gracious also, but that is aside the point for the moment. Your vocabulary in it is right. Your syntax still strays occasionally from the simple order of natural speech.[3]

> Objectivity and again objectivity, and expression: no hindside-beforeness, no straddled adjectives (as

59

"addled mosses dank"), no Tennysonianness of speech; nothing—nothing that you couldn't in some circumstance, in the stress of some emotion, actually say. Every literaryism, every book word, fritters away a scrap of the reader's patience, a scrap of his sense of your sincerity. When one really feels and thinks, one stammers with simple speech; it is only in the flurry, the shallow, frothy excitement of writing, or the inebriety of a metre, that one falls into the easy—oh, how easy!—speech of books and poems that one has read.[4]

Poetry must be *as well written as prose*. Its language must be a fine language, departing in no way from speech save by a heightened intensity (i.e. simplicity).[5]

These passages indicate that Pound esteemed "the simple order of natural speech" as a virtue in poetry, and that the stammer of emotion-choked utterance was not only permissible but desirable in a written poem. If we are to reconcile these principles with Pound's own Cantos, we must conclude that for this writer such simple, emotive speech is by nature more fragmentary and nongrammatical than traditional poetry. It would only be necessary to add the qualification that this fragmentary style may not represent a sharp break with older, more grammatically orthodox poetry. Rather, the peculiarities of elaborate sentences in some important nineteenth-century writers, their exploitation of the dramatic monologue, the variety and effectiveness of occasional fragments in their work—all reveal a kinship with stylistic traits common to major twentieth-century poets and suggest historical continuity in the development of these same traits.

A description of the development of fragmentary structures, however, remains incomplete without a discussion of other tendencies in nineteenth-century poetic idiom which certainly hastened the widespread exploitation of this device. Also, the avant-garde poets of the first quarter of the twentieth century, drawing on foreign literatures and new theories of the nature of the mind's activity, greatly diversified this technique and extended the range and subtlety of its effects. Both the inherent potentialities of English verse and the seminal impact of foreign modes and new ideas must figure in any account of the emergence of the fragment as a primary instrument of poetic expression, but these discussions of external influences on English poetry have been deferred to a later chapter.

That the fragment has so emerged seems indisputable. All but three poets in the later group employ fragmentation as their most common variation in sentence structure. Of these three, two (Yeats and Robinson) are the oldest in this group—both were born before 1870. The other eccentric, Cummings, has almost as many fragmentary as dislocated structures, and the latter, as we have seen, are often oddly like a collection of fragments. Among the earlier poets, on the other hand, only seven of fifteen depend most heavily on fragments; and of these, Emerson and Wilde qualify only because the exclamatory fragment has not been considered a kind of regular sentence. Also, ten of the early poets yielded fewer than 50 fragments in 500 lines, but only four of the later writers had so few. Of the five 1870 poets with the highest proportion of this kind of deviation, four would probably strike us as more "modern" than their contemporaries. Certainly, Whitman, Browning, Dickinson and Hopkins have been recognized as major poets by successive generations, while the reputations of Lowell, Longfellow, Rossetti, and Swinburne have declined.

It is, however, equally indisputable that certain poets of the nineteenth century had already gone far toward making the fragment a complex yet flexible structure. Pound's exceedingly high proportion of fragmentary to

61

regular structures (1.6 to 1) is matched by Whitman's. The elaborate fragment, admittedly more common among the later poets, still occurs in seven writers in the 1870 group. And Whitman has two doubly elaborate fragments, a structure found elsewhere only once, in D. H. Lawrence. Whitman, in fact, seems to have employed most of the kinds of fragments later poets were to exploit.

In part, as selections from some Victorian poets have illustrated, excessive elaboration led to unbalanced sentences; and in these sentences certain nouns, weighty with digressive modifiers, assumed a kind of autonomous force. Thus, many fragments from this period, like this elaborate one from Swinburne, consist of one or two central nouns greatly inflated by adjectival clauses:

> O sleepless heart and sombre soul unsleeping,
> That were athirst for sleep and no more life
> And no more love, for peace and no more strife! [6]

Despite the exclamation point, the distinctive characteristic of this structure is not its explosive passion, but the amount of descriptive material the nouns are made to bear. The dependent adjective clause with its plural verb form serves to unite two potential fragments into a single compound structure, and such clausal elaboration preserves strict grammatical integrity *within* the noun phrase. But in Whitman and for other reasons in Browning, variations appeared that were less clearly a natural evolution of the poetic dialect of the time.

Whitman's "catalogues," for example, very often grow out of a sentence framework; but these great heaps of nouns and noun phrases more than unbalance that framework—they effectively unhinge it. A reader can only superficially distinguish one of these immense sentences from other blocs of clearly independent fragments. Sometimes, indeed, the sense of the passage depends on our ability to dissociate items in the catalogue from the context of the sentence. Consider this stanza from section four of *Song of Myself:*

> Trippers and askers surround me
> People I meet, the effect upon me of my early life
>   or the ward and city I live in, or the nation,
> The latest dates, discoveries, inventions, societies,
>   authors old and new,
> My dinner, dress, associates, looks, compliments,
>   dues,
> The real or fancied indifference of some man or
>   woman I love,
> The sickness of one of my folks or of myself, or ill-
>   doing or loss or lack of money, or depressions
>   or exaltations,
> Battles, horrors of fratricidal war, the fever of
>   doubtful news, the fitful events;
> These come to me days and nights and go from me
>   again,
> But they are not the Me myself.[7]

If we suppose each of these 24 nouns or noun phrases acts as a subject of the verbs "come" and "go," and if we assume that an especially retentive reader is capable of comprehending all these subjects simultaneously, then we must try to make sense of such absurd or laughable statements as "My dinner [and] dress . . . come to me days and nights and go from me again." Surely the reader is not meant to integrate all the disparate references gathered here into a structure made single and coherent by strict syntactic conventions. Rather, some of the first nouns in the sequence—how many one can but guess—probably belong with the first sentence, "Trippers and askers surround me"; of the others a few are nearly free, and the rest could be described, figuratively at least, as "coming and going" in the author's field of experience.

63

This sort of expansion, an accretion by simple addition of nouns in parallel series, seems capable of developing easily into a kind of fragmentation. And throughout *Leaves of Grass*, of course, Whitman often dispenses with main verbs, even such general and limitless ones as "surround" or "come and go." But whether made up of free, discrete nouns or of others bound to a sentence, these catalogues differ fundamentally from the variety of fragment recorded in Pound. They are very extensive—note the extreme multiple elaborations in the Whitman sample—and they are composed of elements of great diversity. Nouns, noun phrases, nouns to which are appended lengthy adjective clauses—all occur helter-skelter. Semantic bonds do not, generally, unify many of these elements. The only words which do provide some unity to the catalogue quoted are the pronouns and pronominals "I," "me," "my," "myself," certainly very general and indirect links. The implied metaphors in the Pound quotation, those relating leaves flashing in sun to fish scales and ivory in silver to nymphs in water, have no parallel here.

Conversely, the catalogue lends itself also to a highly organized and directed development. Sometimes the series contains not diverse items but a great variety of names for the same thing. In the first case the fragments usually strike one as scattered and as literal, prosaic, or "representational"; in the latter case, metaphor seems likely and unity unavoidable. Thus Whitman writes, in "Song of the Broad-Axe,"

> Weapon shapely, naked, wan,
> Head from the mother's bowels drawn,
> Wooded flesh and metal bone, limb only one and
>   lip only one,
> Gray-blue leaf by red-heat grown, helve produced
>   from a little seed sown,
> Resting the grass amid and upon
> To be lean'd and to lean on.[8]

At least two later poets employ catalogues extensively. Lawrence' use of this device is generally restricted to name substitution.

> Worse than the cry of the new-born,
> A scream,
> A yell,
> A shout,
> A paean,
> A death-agony
> A birth-cry
> A submission,
> All tiny, tiny, far away, reptile under the first
> dawn.[9]

Sandburg, however, sometimes displays catholic diversity:

> Hog Butcher for the World
> Tool Maker, Stacker of Wheat,
> Player with Railroads and the Nation's Freight
> Handler;
> Stormy, husky, brawling,
> City of the Big Shoulders:
> They tell me you are wicked and I believe them,
> for I have seen your painted women under the
> gas lamps luring the farm boys.[10]

Battering rams, blind mules, mounted policemen, trucks hauling caverns of granite, elephants grappling gorillas in a death strange, cathedrals, arenas, platforms, somersaults of telescoped railroad train wrecks, exhausted egg heads, piles of skulls, mountains of empty sockets, mummies of kings and mobs, memories of work gangs and wrecking crews, sobs of winds and water storms, all frozen and held on paths leading on to spirals of new zigzags—[11]

65

In general, the loose catalogues like the last one do not possess visible links relating individual elements in the series; whether such conglomerations do in fact possess any structure is an obvious problem which we shall have occasion to return to later. In the other passages, on the other hand, strong semantic bonds are reinforced by grammatical endings (*-er* making analogous nouns of verbs like "stack," "handle") or parallel construction ("*A scream, A shout . . .*") or even repetition of words and cognates ("cry of the new born," "birth-cry"). A catalogue of various alternative names, however, is still at most a linear series of simple metaphors, one term of which the reader knows. Like a litany, the catalogue often is an extended description and decoration which gives substance to a general concept; but seldom does one discover in Sandburg or Lawrence the complex binding and patterning of fragments manifest in Pound's poetry.

Besides such simple descriptive and representational fragments, Whitman composed the first of what I have labeled "fused" structures, using fragments as the chief bonding mechanism. Here his successors are many: Crane, Stevens, Eliot, and Pound all furnish examples of such structures. A fused structure consists of a word or group of words whose meaning and/or grammatical form could integrate the word or words into either of two other discrete structures. Such fusion very often has the effect of confusing traditional syntactic relations, as if to allow the word group with multiple function to oscillate ambiguously between its possible contexts.

> Now while I sat in the day and look'd forth,
> In the close of the day with its light and the fields
>   of spring, and the farmers preparing their
>   crops,
> In the large unconscious scenery of my land with
>   its lakes and forests,

> In the heavenly aerial beauty, (after the perturb'd
>   winds and the storms)
> Under the arching heavens of the afternoon swift
>   passing, and the voices of children and
>   women,
> The many-moving sea tides, and I saw the ships
>   how they sail'd,
> And the summer approaching with richness, and
>   the fields all busy with labor, and the infi-
>   nite separate houses, how they all went on,
>   each with its meals and minutia of daily
>   usages. . . .[12]

In this selection the phrase "the farmers preparing their
crops" seems partly independent, going ill enough as
an object of the preposition in the phrase "the day with
its farmers preparing their crops." But the next reference to human beings, "and the voices of children and
women," has even less apparent relation to its context.
"Under the arching heavens of the voices . . ." does
not make perfect sense, yet surely the noun phrase has
no grammatical links with "I saw the ships how they
sailed." How, incidentally, does the poet make a transition from "the fields of spring" or "lakes and forests"
to the sea tides and sailing ships?

If arching heavens suggest choirs of angels, and if
the voices of women and children remind Whitman of
angelic singing, then the noun phrase is linked—de-
viously enough—with preceding phrases. If, on the
other hand, the voices suggest the murmur and rush
of moving sea tides, then the noun phrase is semantically bound to the subsequent phrase and sentence.
"Voices" and "sea tides" remain fragments in any case,
but they may have implicit relations with one another
and with neighboring structures.

A more readily identifiable form of fusion occurs
when the ambivalent structure can be related grammatically and with equal facility to alternative struc-

tures. Here is a trivial example from Pound's *Hugh Selwyn Mauberley.*

> Beneath the sagging roof
> The stylist has taken shelter,
> Unpaid, uncelebrated,
> At last from the world's welter
> Nature receives him.[13]

The adjectives could belong to either sentence, since the commas fail to mark a clear terminal point. Eliot creates far more intriguing ambiguities in *The Wasteland.*

> At the violet hour, when the eyes and back
> Turn upward from the desk, when the human en-
>   gine waits
> Like a taxi throbbing waiting,
> I Tiresias, though blind, throbbing between two
>   lives,
> Old man with wrinkled female breasts, can see
> At the violet hour, the evening hour that strives
> Homeward, and brings the sailor home from sea,
> The typist home at teatime, clears her breakfast,
>   lights
> Her stove, and lays out food in tins.[14]

> Unreal City,
> Under the brown fog of a winter dawn,
> A crowd flowed over London Bridge, so many,
> I had not thought death had undone so many.[15]

The noun phrase "so many" stands between two sentences with which it has strong and simultaneous affinities. "Many" and "crowd" are nearly synonyms, and an appositive noun phrase modifying a subject is often displaced to the end of the sentence. However, the phrase is repeated literally in the second sentence, and appositive modifiers are also commonly displaced from a position adjacent to a noun object, usually standing last in the sentence, to the very beginning of the structure (Hamlet's "My father—methinks I see my father"). One simply cannot determine the function of the phrase in terms of traditional grammar. Quite probably Eliot intended to leave the reader no choice but the obvious one of considering the bracketing sentences and the intervening phrase as a single structure.

The first passage confuses customary grammatical relations even more radically. "The typist home at tea-time" can act both as an object of the verb "brings" and as a subject of the verb "clears." Again, commas appear where one expects periods or an absence of punctuation, so that sentences have no clear boundaries. A simple relative pronoun ("who clears") would have prevented such confusion. Even more strongly than in the case of the ambiguous "so many," one suspects that the poet has deliberately blurred the lines of division between sentences, or between "thoughts." Still, Eliot prefers fusion by overt grammatical linkage, rather than by the more tenuous semantic relations which operate in Whitman.

In many ways, Hart Crane profited from the innovations of these poets, both of whom he revered. Some of his fused structures seem to be a combination of the characteristic techniques of the two. In this passage (an eulogy of Walt Whitman), Crane balances a long series of phrases between a pronoun fragment and a simple statement.

> Thou, there beyond—
> Glacial sierras and the flight of ravens,
> Hermetically past condor zones, through zenith
>   havens
> Past where the albatross has offered up

His last wing-pulse, and downcast as a cup
That's drained, is shivered back to earth—thy
    wand
Has beat a song, O Walt,—there and beyond! [16]

The phrases which intervene between "thou" and "thy wand" could be associated with either, yet the noun with its pronominal modifier and the pronoun themselves have a grammatical bond, though not in the context of any realized sentence. The repetition of "there" and "beyond" in proximity to these key nominals links them indirectly. However, to associate the phrases with "thou" one must make "glacial sierras" an object of the preposition "beyond"—here too punctuation seriously hinders such an easy reading—and then, the second "beyond" being adverbial, grammatical parallelism is destroyed. But the alternative is to consider "sierras" and "flight" as additional free fragments only associated with the following phrases by virtue of meaning. Again, to attempt to force the words into mutually exclusive syntactic molds probably defeats the poet's intention and perhaps weakens the effect of the whole.

Portions of *The Bridge*, especially the "tunnel" section, introduce a variation, somewhat like fusion, in which a sentence at first coherent disintegrates into fragments. Unlike the elaborate sentence whose sheer length and complexity often encourage the reader to ingest it bit by bit, some of Crane's disintegrating sentences are brief, and their fragmentation sudden and deliberate.

Stick your patent name on a signboard brother—
    allover—going west—young man
Tintex—Japalac—Certain-teed Overalls ads and
    lands sakes! under the new playbill ripped in
    the guaranteed corner—see Bert Williams
    what? [17]

Here the words separated by dashes include adverbs, adjectives, and several nouns which could conceivably belong in the opening sentence. However, the ordering of these words argues against such integration. None except the first, "allover," would ordinarily occur at the end of the sentence, particularly as one of a series of nonparallel modifiers.

An understanding of the relations between the fragments in this series depends in part on our recollection of their clearer relations in another context. The words "going west—young man" of course come from Greeley's famous injunction, which could apply ironically to salesmen of Crane's time. "Tintex," "Japalac," and "Certain-teed Overalls" probably are printed on the same labels with the word "patent," so that all are associated in some fashion with "name on a signboard." The final question, "see Bert Williams what," if it is to be linked to preceding word groups, involves the reader in rather ingenious speculation. "Ripped in the guaranteed corner" seems to belong with "Certain-teed Overalls," but since Bert Williams was a well-known Negro comedian, the playbill probably advertizes a coming vaudeville show, and, plastered over the overalls ad, which has been torn, leads the recording consciousness of the poem to contemplate attending the show. If the ad read "See Bert Williams!", the silent question "See Bert Williams *what?*" is a likely response; or, perhaps part of a sentence is torn off, leaving "See Bert Williams. . . ." If Williams' costume was one of rags and patches, the phrase "ripped in the guaranteed corner" would also serve to make the transition from one subject to the next. According to this interpretation, the passage moves, without any grammatical signaling of such a shift, from the blanketing generalities of "allover" and "young man" to a particular person's idle musing.

As in the fragments quoted from Eliot and Whitman, Crane depends on the reader to recognize not only the meaning of his words, but also the possible contexts in which they have occurred. Only thus, in fact, can the reader hope to unify sequences of fragments without grammatical or obvious semantic links. It is obvious that "Bert Williams" has no meaning clearly and immediately connected to the concept of Tintex or Certainteed overalls, or to the command "Go West, young man." Such complete disintegration of syntactic forms presupposes more than ingenuity on the part of the reader. A reader must also possess a background of experience similar to that of the poet's. What if a reader were unfamiliar with brand names and patenting regulations and with the American habit of reading and reacting to billboards? If he did not recognize Greeley's words and the irony of their echo here? Surely the passage would baffle him. Unlike the catalogue, wherein fragments usually only describe, and unlike fusion, wherein a fragment may perform two simultaneous but determined roles, the disintegrating sentence produces fragments associated very subtly—even obscurely—to one another and to surrounding structures

Another and less pervasive sort of fragment seems to derive more or less clearly from the traditional "absolute phrase." Such phrases, common enough in Latin, appear throughout English poetry, as here in Scott's "Lay of the Last Minstrel":

> All loose her negligent attire, all loose her golden hair,
> Hung Margarot o'er her slaughtered sire. . . .[18]

Ordinarily, the phrase is formed by attaching a noun and its participial modifier to a sentence pattern of which they form no essential part. However, an obvious association exists between the absolute phrase and some word in the sentence. Sometimes the association is reinforced by a grammatical bond like the pronoun "her" in the lines from Scott. But when such associations and bonds are absent, the absolute phrase becomes almost indistinguishable from a fragment. (Compare "All sails furled, the ship glided into the bay," and "Ducks broiling, the ship glided into the bay.") Often, in the course of compiling the data for twentieth-century poets, I found it very difficult to decide whether an "association" of some kind warranted classifying a phrase as an absolute one. Such uncertainty suggests that, without even a change of form, this structure could change its function from that of a clear modifier to that of a fragment bound very tenuously and indirectly to an accompanying sentence.

Such a transformation could have been much abetted by the use of absolute phrases in the Browning dramatic monologue. Obviously, the almost cryptic brevity, the variability of position, and the simplicity of structure of the phrase bear a resemblance to laconic speech or provide a literary illusion of spoken idiom. One thinks immediately of certain common expressions which could serve as models for such structures: "All done!" (as an answer to a question or as a general announcement) "His crops failing that way, he had to sell out." At any rate, Browning fashioned such phrases often (my italics):

> *Just a spirt*
> *O' the proper fiery acid o'er its face,*
> And forth the alloy unfastened flies in fume;
> While, self-sufficient now, the shape remains,
> The rondure brave, the lilied loveliness,
> Gold as it was, is, shall be evermore:
> Prime nature with an added artistry—
> *No carat lost,* and you have gained a ring.[19]

These variations from traditional literary syntax are not restricted, however, to colloquial and highly emotive styles. A group of absolute noun phrases crops out in the midst of this otherwise straitlaced sentence of Morris.

Ah! through the hush the looked-for midnight
    clangs!
And then, e'en while its last stroke's solemn drone
In the cold air by unlit windows hangs,
Out break the bells above the year foredone,
Change, kindness lost, love left unloved alone;
Till their despairing sweetness makes thee deem
Thou once wert loved, if but amidst a dream.[20]

"Change," "kindness lost," and "love" erupt in the sentence as broad concepts felt to be related to the ringing of bells. But the poet leaves the relation unspecified, indistinct. Both in formal and colloquial poetry, the kinship between the conventional absolute phrase and the noun phrase as independent element provides additional evidence of historical continuity in the formation of one of modern poetry's most salient traits of style.

When clearly broken away from a sentence pattern, the absolute phrase may resemble a descriptive fragment of the kind common to catalogues. Concrete, highly visual, static, such phrases can, with utmost economy, locate a scene or fix details of decor. Poems in the early decades of the twentieth century sometimes began thus:

Clearing in the forest,
In the wild Kentucky forest,
And the stars, wintry stars strewn above! [21]

Apple-green west and an orange bar;
And the crystal eye of a lone, one star. . . .[22]

The purely descriptive fragment evolved, among some "Imagistes," into elliptic, rather complex metaphor. But the essential characteristics of the structure remained constant: a *concrete* noun is generally indispensable as "head" of the structure; such nouns often occur in the

74

company of others of similarly independent cast; and the relation of one descriptive fragment to another may be unspecified by signals of grammar or punctuation. When so separated from an orthodox syntactic pattern, however, the noun phrase may lose the appearance of a colloquialism. Certainly a long series of fragments, like Pound's cited earlier, hardly forms part of an ordinary conversation or even of a monologue.

But when an independent noun or group of nouns with attendant modifiers remains implicitly associated with or buried within an otherwise coherent structure, one suspects that the poet is exploiting a unique dimension of this device. Already, in remarks on Browning's dislocation by interruption—and especially the interruption of fragments—it has been suggested that this poet attempts to reproduce not only the *spoken* but also the play of the *perceived* and *conceived* material of the mind. A poet may, in short, go a step beyond monologue to interior monologue and reverie—with a corresponding decay of formal syntax. To abandon the sentence mold entirely for long stretches, as many imagist poets habitually did, would not create a realistic transcript of this psychic content. An unbroken series of elegant periods is, of course, equally unlikely. The structure of a language is, after all, neither the rational imposition of presumptive theoreticians nor a heap of raw words. Language is thought itself. It is born, bent, and broken by the mind of all, but according to the whim of each. One would expect, then, some sentences—thought on the verge of utterance—some parts of sentences to represent those half-formed or abandoned thoughts of which writers speak and the verbal equivalents of sense impressions, which are, one assumes, the stuff out of which thought is by some mysterious process created.

The "disintegrating" sentence follows such a recipe; and in passages from Thomas, Eliot, and William Carlos Williams, as in Whitman and Crane, one often discovers a shift from the easy, natural order of colloquial speech to an erratic sprinkling of fragments and back again. Sometimes, as earlier examples indicate, the absolute phrase with fading relevance to a sentence acts as a kind of bridge to make the shift unobtrusive. Relevance, at the same time, depends less and less on grammatical signals and becomes almost solely a matter of semantic resonances, loosely controlled "associations."

At other times, the shift is abrupt. But so, often, is the transition from speech to thought or from careful thought to tangential musing. Witness Graves' lines from "The Halls of Bedlam."

> No one could stop him,
> No one understood;
> And in the evening papers. . . .

> (Imminent genius,
> Troubles at the office,
> Normally, normally,
> As if already mad.) [23]

Here, adverbs, as well as nouns, appear disjoined from any sentence. It would indeed seem unsafe to suppose that the mind produces fragments of only one variety. Once the main subject of these structures has been identified as an "imminent genius," Graves evokes no more details about the person. He strives to render a partially articulated apprehension of the unusual relation between man and act; he traces a swift and ironic association between the subject's apparent *manner* of doing something ("normally") and the actual condition ("as if already mad") normal behavior implies in such a person—suppressing any mention of particular deeds.

The overwhelming predominance of the noun fragment in modern poetry is probably due to that structure's aptness in representing, often in a single word or phrase, isolated visual images of a particular shape, size, and color: "a chocolate," "a mouse," "straw hat." A good part of psychic life—dreams, reverie, imaginative creation—unfolds as a procession of such images. From these, more elaborate structures may develop. Sometimes development is nearly complete; sometimes, as in the selection from Graves, it is rudimentary. A poetry which strives to model itself after spontaneous psychic patterns would reflect several stages of such development. It would range from spare noun phrases—raw sense impressions—through groups of coalescing images to coherent, though swift-paced, laconic and colloquial sentences.

It is clear, then, that the modern poet's penchant for fragmentary structures may involve also a tendency toward a colloquial style, a style whose characteristic sentences are simple and regular. After a closer study of the latter tendency, we shall consider how these two movements may be related. It is equally apparent that the development of the fragment is a complex matter: the representational fragment in Whitman's catalogues and the descriptive fragment common to early imagist poets differ in structure and function from Eliot's fusions and Crane's disintegrating sentences

The length and diversity of many catalogues, the apparently deliberate syntactic ambiguities of fusion, and the sharp and sudden disintegration of some sentences make clear that the fragment did not simply evolve from a Victorian taste for langorous overelaboration. In fact, as employed by the early imagistes (Aldington, Flint, Pound, H. D., D. H. Lawrence) most fragmentary structures were expressions of a revolt against nineteenth-century stylistic mannerisms. However, as a study of elaboration and the absolute phrase indicates, poets of the first three decades of the century unwittingly furthered tendencies which had appeared in their unfashionable forerunners. At the same time, the credit for increasing the flexibility of fragmentary structures must go largely to innovators like Whitman and Browning, who overstrained and broke the traditional syntactic molds of English poetry.

PLAIN TALK

WE HAVE NOTICED that certain poets tend to write, in the same compositions, large numbers of fragments in addition to regular sentences. It should not be inferred that fragmentation always accompanies a rebounding to regularity at the expense of other kinds of variation. The two tendencies may even be coincidental, though this possibility is not a likely one. At least, a style consistently regular can exist without much fragmentation: Frost seldom varies from a natural order, and he does not show a marked preference for any of the three sorts of innovations discussed here. When extreme, such syntactic regularity in poetry becomes a kind of variation itself. Thus poets in the late 1920s and early 1930s to some extent distinguish themselves from their predecessors by a preference for the plain, regular ways of saying something.

Evidence for this claim does not appear obviously in the table, where the apportionment of regular structures in each body of samples seems to be fairly consistent, most of the poets in both groups writing about 100–150 regular sentences for each 500 lines. It is worth noting, however, that except for Tennyson and Emerson, none of the earlier writers had more than 170 regular structures (Wilde is only one short of this figure), while five of the twentieth-century poets exceeded this figure. On the other hand Swinburne and Browning had less than 100 such structures, but of the later poets only Robinson—again, the oldest of his group—had so few.

The *degree* to which these 30 poets alter structure, whatever the kind of alteration, does not at first seem to suggest a historical pattern. In both groups, some alter much, some little. But the proportion of secondary and tertiary variations is lower among the more recent poets. If we exclude the primary mode of syntactic variation in each individual case (dislocation in Longfellow and fragmentation in Whitman, for example) and add up for each poet the remaining number of irregular structures, we find that for eight of the nineteenth-century poets this total exceeds 50, while in only three instances do the later poets surpass this limit. Also, the very minimum sum of secondary and tertiary variations in the 1870 group (Bryant's) is 27, a figure twice equaled, by Lawrence and Pound, and twice outdone in samples from the 1930 group (Stevens, 26; Williams, 17).

Because of the uneven number of lines in these samples, however, the proportion indexes are undoubtedly the best indicators of the degree of regularity to be found in an author's style. These indexes are determined by dividing the number of regular constructions in each author into the number of each of his two most common kinds of variation. Adding primary and secondary index numbers, found in the column "Dominant Types" in Appendix I, we find that the highest totals of these numbers occur before 1900: Whitman, 2.03; Longfellow, 1.57; Hopkins, 1.42; Browning, 1.39; as compared with Pound, 1.76; Lawrence, 1.12; Williams, 1.10; H. D., 1.08. If we consider only the proportion of secondary variations to regular structures, this proportion generally runs lower for poets after Wilde. In six cases the index number is less than .15. Only Arnold and Hardy—the latter one of the youngest of his group —display a comparable conservatism. Thus, though it may grow more violent and more idiosyncratic at the hands of twentieth-century poets, syntactic variation may become less common.

Certain stylistic profiles based on a strict regularity appear in the group of recent poets. Frost phrases his thoughts in a remarkably regular way. No other poet in this study wrote such a high proportion of sentences according to conventional models. Others, however, also vary their patterns seldom and rely on no particular kind of variation at the expense of other kinds. Yeats first, then Frost, Sandburg, and, to a lesser degree, Eliot exhibit this tendency. Accordingly, the sentences of the first three in this list are likely to be natural, uncomplicated, and coherent. In Frost's "The Cow in Apple Time" seven out of eight sentences are regular:

> Something inspires the only cow of late
> To make no more of a wall than an open gate,
> And think no more of wall-builders than fools.
> Her face is flecked with pomace and she drools
> A cider syrup. Having tasted fruit,
> She scorns a pasture withering to the root.
> She runs from tree to tree where lie and sweeten
> The windfalls spiked with stubble and worm-eaten.
> She leaves them bitten when she has to fly.
> She bellows on a knoll against the sky.
> Her udder shrivels and the milk goes dry.[24]

It is apparent from the chart that a few earlier writers fashioned for themselves a similar idiom. Bryant and Emerson, Hardy and Wilde also cultivated the virtues of simplicity, normality, even terseness. Bryant and Wilde may seem out of place here; but the former's lines illustrate how a truly classic restraint respects the innate character of a language; and, despite Wilde's professed love of frills, his later poetry has the easy, unadorned grace of ballad or ditty rather than the rococo one might expect. Consider the octave of the sonnet "Santa Decca":

> The Gods are dead: no longer do we bring
>   To grey-eyed Pallas crowns of olive-leaves!

Demeter's child no more hath tithe of sheaves,
And in the noon the careless shepherds sing,
For Pan is dead, and all the wantoning
　　By secret glade and devious haunt is o'er:
　　Young Hylas seeks the water-springs no more;
Great Pan is dead, and Mary's Son is King.[25]

Emerson and Hardy, on the other hand, would seem a likely pair of predecessors for a poetry of down to-earth speech. Both were more prolific in prose than in poetry. Both wrote of "common" or universal man. Both, optimist and pessimist, directed their messages to the public at large. Here again, tracing the development of this current of colloquialism, one is forced to recognize that recent poets are indebted to their immediate forerunners, who pruned and straightened some of the exotic growths of poetry in their century. Untermeyer thus begins his anthology of *Modern American Poetry* with selections from Emily Dickinson, saying in the introduction,

> And with the use of the material of everyday life, there came a further simplification: the use of the language of everyday speech. The stilted and mouth-filling phrases were practically discarded in favor of the daily vocabulary. . . . As the speech of the modern poet grew less elaborate, so did the patterns embodying it. Not necessarily discarding rhyme, regular rhythm or any of the musical assets of the older poets, forms grew simpler; the intricate versification gave way to lines that reflect and suggest the tones of animated and even exalted speech.[26]

Already in Pound's remarks on poetry as speech under the stress of emotion, we have seen that this drift toward regularity was not an unconscious one. Pound was seconded by Yeats, who rewrote his early, ornate poems. As Thomas Parkinson observes, Yeats revised not only in order to freshen his diction, but also in order to simplify and regularize—according to the common patterns of English—his syntax.[27] Lawrence, too, wanted a poetry stripped of all arabesques.[28] Eliot, and Crane, Auden, and Williams after him, often transcribe bits of dialogue, snatches of song or lines from a poster directly into the body of a poem; hence, "HURRY UP PLEASE ITS TIME." Or they introduce such material with an ironic twist: "O O O O that Shakespearian Rag —/It's so elegant/So intelligent." Generally this foreign matter in the poem is in the form of simple fragments or short, regular utterances. Here, too, the poet must be selecting material consciously, so that these continual flashes of dialogue or chatty near-dialogue—the term would apply often if only the reader had an opportunity to answer the poet—offer proof that some modern poets try, literally, to say something or to reflect what others say, rather than to write *about* what they feel. One may strongly suspect that the novel, too, has moved from extended descriptions purveyed second hand of the characters' "thoughts" and "feelings" (Eliot, Hardy, Conrad) to a heavier reliance on dramatic dialogue— or, eventually, interior monologue—as a means of revealing passion and intent (Hemingway, Joyce).

At the same time, it would be a gross oversimplification to assert that modern poets simply imitate contemporary speech. In the section dealing with fragmentation are examples of poetry striving to reflect the content of the mind at the "pre-speech" level. Logically enough, other poets write at a "post-speech" level; that is, they polish and reshape crude utterance into patterns of a greater variability, yet always taking care to avoid grandiloquence. Auden is such a poet; so is Yeats—he seems on the precise knife edge between the colloquial and the literary—and so on occasions are Eliot and Pound, Graves and Thomas.

Of course, as a glance at the "General Prologue" to

The Canterbury Tales establishes, poets long ago managed to fuse successfully literary embellishment and easy, natural grace. However, the relative emphasis poets assign to these two stylistic poles—simple against elaborate, natural against contorted—may tell us to what degree art is responsive to certain forces in its environment, those of court and country, for example. But before embarking on such attractive and dangerous speculations, we merely note that between 1870 and 1930 major poets tended to simplify and regularize their sentences to make them conform, sometimes rather closely, to the patterns of everyday speech. Their variations tend to be of one kind, fragmentation; and while for some the propensity for this kind is often excessive, others revert to a regular English word order without undue encumbrances (pace, Cummings).

4

The Strange and the Familiar

HOPKINS AND YEATS

TURNING NOW to the work of individuals, we find that a few nineteenth-century poets introduced the syntactic variations which many modern poets have especially exploited; while on the other hand a few modern poets modified rather than revolutionized the syntax of their Victorian predecessors. In this chapter the poetry of Gerard Manley Hopkins supplies some examples of the kind of radical syntactic innovation, especially fragmentation, found in some modern poetry; while an analysis of selections from Yeats illustrates how Victorian mannerisms were curbed and modulated to strengthen another basic characteristic of modern verse, its regularity. Then, lines from another pair of writers, Browning and T. S. Eliot, have been examined in order to demonstrate the range and use of these salient traits of modern poetic syntax, fragmentation and colloquial regularity, in specific poems. Despite the many striking differences between the styles of these two poets, it is possible to see the structure of Eliot's "sentences" as an extension of, rather than a departure from, certain of Browning's techniques. The two poets use the fragment, for example, for similar purposes.

The syntactic variations favored in most nineteenth-

84

century verse do not, as quotations in chapter 2 illustrate, make poems difficult to understand. The work of Browning and Hopkins, on the other hand, has often been called "difficult," as has that of Eliot and Yeats. Since all these poets have gained a certain notoriety for an alleged "difficulty" or "obscurity," and all are in some way representative of tendencies in modern poetry, in this discussion of their work I have sought to determine how, precisely, unorthodox syntax may battle the reader.

Hopkins and Yeats illustrate strikingly the two tendencies remarkable in many modern poets. Certainly, Hopkins' innovations—many of his sentences simply cannot be forced into familiar categories—mark him as more than a mere forerunner of later experimentation. But even when these unusual structures are excepted, his style distinguishes him clearly from his contemporaries and associates him with later poets. Yeats, on the other hand, exhibits few structural peculiarities, and this very orthodoxy links him with another movement in modern poetry, that toward plain or even colloquial statement; at the same time, a modest preference for dislocation and elaboration betrays his early admiration for his immediate predecessors: Morris, Rossetti, and Swinburne.

An analysis of 500 lines of the work of each man confirms that Hopkins is by far the more varied stylist. In a total of 324 sentences there are 220 variations from the standard pattern, a ratio of about three to two. Out of Yeats's 172 sentences, slightly more than one-third are unusual. Also, the Yeats poems analyzed contain only five discrete structures which vary in more than one way, while all of the Hopkins poems contain several structures which may be both fragmentary and elaborate, or which may be dislocated at more than one point. There are 40 such duplications in the sample, 26 in the *Wreck of the Deutschland* alone. Dislocation and elaboration, for example, converge in these lines:

85

> She to the black-about air, to the breaker, the
>   thickly
> Falling flakes, to the throng that catches and quails
>   Was calling 'O Christ, Christ, come
>   quickly'. . . .[1]

Probably the large number of elaborate constructions
in Yeats, contrasted with the scarcity of that device in
Hopkins, indicates that Yeats preferred to expand
rather than to rearrange sentence forms. Consider the
lengthy first sentence of "The Dawn":

> I would be ignorant as the dawn
> That has looked down
> On that old queen measuring a town
> With the pin of a brooch,
> Or on the withered men that saw
> From their pedantic Babylon
> The careless planets in their courses,
> The stars fade out where the moon comes,
> And took their tablets and did sums. . . .[2]

Hopkins, on the other hand, creates structures which
are complex and often unique without always being
elaborate as the term is here defined. Of his 115 fragments, for example, only twelve are of the traditional
exclamatory sort, and only eight are colloquial abbrevia-
tions. To call the remainder "descriptive" would be to
identify them only very imperfectly; too many maintain
dynamic force through subordinate elements containing verbs or verbal modifiers.

> Not a dooms-day dazzle in his coming nor dark
>   as he came;
> Kind, but royally reclaiming his own. . . .[3]

Also, few of the dislocations in Hopkins result from the
exigencies of a rhyme scheme. Hopkins' theory of

"sprung rhythm" may be partially responsible for the inordinate number and original cast of these dislocations, but given his view that "it is the rhythm of common speech and written prose" and that "it is found in nursery rhymes, weather saws, and so on,"[4] one can hardly claim that metrical patterns necessarily distort the syntax of his sentences.

If one examines these samples closely, however, they yield implications that go beyond a simple confirmation of the expected. It can be demonstrated that the unique kinds of fragmentation and dislocation that Hopkins prefers often entail obscurity, whatever the words themselves may signify; whereas Yeats makes statements almost impossible to misconstrue, though they may be difficult to understand, and whatever problems his work may present to the reader stem from his choice of words and figures rather than from their arrangement. Yeats's "unusual" sentences, in most of the poems considered here, are not strikingly different from constructions found traditionally in English poetry. Their structure may be elaborate, but it is merely a replication of standard patterns. Fragments occur rarely and are almost always either colloquial or exclamatory. The few dislocations also appear to be simple inversions of fundamental elements for the sake of rhyme or metrical grace. But Hopkins contorts or cuts off sentences more often than not; that is to say, much more often than Yeats does. Some of his fragments are more complex, more elaborate, than most sentences. Some of the dislocations are unprecedented and involve such odd innovations as the interruption of single words or of phrase patterns by displaced modifying elements.

The one short poem, "The Nightingale," selected from Hopkins' early works, departs radically from the style of the *Deutschland*. The sentences in it are mostly of regular pattern, the innovations rigidly conventional. Even this cursory comparison suggests that his style after 1875 becomes truly "original, spare, and strange," that the poet determined to wrench his language into intricate and unique forms. "The Nightingale" (January 18, 1866) contains 16 regular structures out of a total of 23 sentences, and only one fragment. But by 1879, when "The Bugler's First Communion" was written, Hopkins was composing two or three abnormal sentences for every regular one. The proportion persists in the two long poems analyzed.

This wrenching of language, this displacement and omission of the parts of a sentence, invites ambiguity and sometimes obscurity. "Nightingale" is a poem easy to understand; the difficulty of construing many poems after 1875 is notorious. One of the complex or elaborate fragments from the *Deutschland*, for example, might be read as a sentence.

> past all
> Grasp God, throned behind
> Death with a sovereignty that heeds but hides,
> bodes but abides;
> With a mercy that outrides
> The all of water, an ark
> For the listener. . . .[5]

The structure has five certain verbs, but it is possible that "grasp" is a sixth in the imperative mood. However, the trace of inept vagueness in the phrase "past all" makes this reading less likely than that which would make "grasp" a noun object of the preposition. If a fragment, however, the structure must also be counted elaborate and dislocated; for it contains five finite verbs and the adjectival phrase "past all grasp" would normally follow a noun. To mark each of these variations does not truly reflect the uniqueness of their convergence, and does not take into account at all the ambiguous reading.

Occasionally this ambiguity is unresolvable and odd syntax directly fosters obscurity, if one accepts uncertain sense as one of the meanings of that term. This problem appears in these lines from "The Bugler's First Communion":

> Let me though see no more of him, and not
>   disappointment
> Those sweet hopes quell whose least me
>   quickenings lift,
> In scarlet or somewhore of some day seeing
>   That brow and bead of being,
> An our day's God's own Galahad.[6]

The function of the noun "disappointment" hovers between that of displaced object of the verb "quell" and subject of the same verb used as a complementary infinitive of the modal auxiliary "let." Reshuffled according to these two readings the sentence would read

1. Do not let disappointment quell those sweet hopes . . . of some day seeing . . . Galahad . . . somewhere . . . in scarlet.
2. Those sweet hopes . . . of some day seeing . . . etc. . . . quell not disappointment. . . .

These two fundamentally contradictory interpretations, however, are further complicated by the ambiguity of the function of the phrase "of some day seeing/ That brow and bead of being," which could possibly modify "disappointment." Shifting this modifier would reverse the sense of the first reading and considerably alter that of the second. On grammatical grounds, the first reconstruction seems certainly the most likely, since, if we suppress intervening word groups, "of some day seeing" follows directly upon "hopes"—the normal idiomatic pattern. But one is left with nagging doubts. Would not then the final injunction, an expression of the hope of seeing the bugler "in scarlet or somewhere," cancel the first, an injunction that "no more of him" be seen? Hopkins may mean that he wishes not to know of the earthly fate of the new convert, who may stray from the faith, but hopes to meet him in heaven. Such a reading, if satisfactory, is but barely so, for the image of an "our day's" Galahad in scarlet dress suggests an earthly—even a militant British—rather than a divine splendor. Surely the lines make better sense if we treat "of some day seeing" as a radically displaced complement of "disappointment," whatever violence is done to the expected sequence of sentence elements. Finally, the placement of the modifiers "in scarlet" and "somewhere" permits some additional quibbling. If the two elements are attached to "of some day seeing," the resulting implication would differ much from that obtained by placing them after "Galahad."

Thus, there are at least four possible interpretations of the lines, to which one may assign varying degrees of probability, and a couple of equally possible minor variations on these interpretations. Again, to record this construction as three dislocations is to provide no hint of its unique quality. Such daring disjointings as "brim, in a flash, full"; "I found it, a winter and warm"; or "brown-as-dawning-skinned" are likewise only inadequately classified as dislocations.

Despite such singularity of style, Hopkins' poetry can with profit be contrasted to that of poets nearer the standard. Sometimes the difficulty of a passage seems to be a function of (1) the number of syntactic variations from regular patterns per given number of structures and per individual structure and (2) the kinds of variation. In the lines from Hopkins employed in this analysis, none of the regular constructions baffles a reader very much. It is the elaborate fragment, the sentence dislocated in two or three places, and the phrase split into parts by another phrase that give pause, or puzzle. To a far lesser degree, other poets, most notably Eliot, exhibit this same correlation between syntactic variation in a passage and the difficulty a reader may have in comprehending it. But irresolvable obscurity, as the following chapters suggest, is

likely to be a product of both odd semantic and uncertain syntactic relations.

Of course Hopkins was aware that his preoccupation
with music and metrics, with poetry fashioned for
recital "as by nature verse should be," [7] did violence
to his syntax. In commenting on the tortured sonnet
"Harry Ploughman" he writes to Robert Bridges, "The
difficulties are of syntax no doubt. Dividing a compound word by a clause sandwiched into it was a
desperate deed, I feel, and I do not feel that it was
an unquestionable success." [8] Hopkins' motive for seeking whatever strange beauty he won at the risk of gro-
tesqueness does not, however, concern this study of the
consequences of his method. Later poets were to achieve
similar effects by like techniques, but working from
much different prejudices. Mallarmé, entranced with
words and their inner music, suffered them to twist and
break the sentence. The imagists, indirectly and imperfectly imitating oriental poetry, hoped to invest the
striking phrase with more force than the qualified statement. Breton and the surrealists valued and tried to
capture the incoherent eruptions of the unconscious. In
all these diverse waves of experiment, abnormal syntax
is responsible for both spectacular successes and irritat-
ing failures.

Yeats has been accused of obscurity too, and as in
Hopkins' case, it is a commonplace to observe that his
very early poems are not remarkable either for their
originality or for their difficulty. The sample examined
here draws one long poem from the poet's work at mid-
career, the rest from *The Tower*, where some of his
sternest demands on readers are made. The syntax of
the earlier poem, "In Memory of Major Robert Gregory,"
is indistinguishable from that of the later ones. All the
poems, in fact, whatever problems they may raise or
whatever value we may assign to them, exhibit great
uniformity of syntax. Regular structures always predominate over all variations taken together. The num-

ber of fragments, always small, is about equal to the number of dislocations, while there are usually a few more elaborate constructions than any other sort of variation. Further, most of the fragments and dislocations are of a conventional type, and no unique ramifications of them were recorded.

Here, for example, is one of the structures scored as a fragment:

> Never had I more excited, passionate, fantastical
> Imagination, nor an ear and eye
> That more expected the impossible—
> No, not in boyhood when with rod and fly,
> Or the humbler worm, I climbed Ben Bulben's
> back. . . .[9]

The complex of phrases and clauses following "no" could of course be considered an idiomatic extension of the adverb of negation in the preceding sentence, forming an elaborate sentence with one dislocation. However, "no," itself ordinarily a sentence, intervenes, and along with the dash, isolates the structure sufficiently to allow it to be catalogued as a fragment. It is nevertheless easy to see that this fragment is much more obviously bound to its context than are the scraps of phrases in *The Waste Land* or the *Cantos,* and that its idiomatic flavor contrasts sharply with the tone of some of Hopkins' fragments. The first words of Hopkins' line, "Where, where was a, where was a place," have no apparent grammatical value in any sentence. The *wheres* are linked by commas to a sentence, as Yeats's phrase is by a dash, but they do not modify or supply meaning as the Yeats structure does. A reading of the Hopkins line aloud can make clear that it is broken speech and may be considered two fragments followed by a complete sentence.

Another common kind of variant occurs in this passage:

And followed up those baying creatures towards—
O towards I have forgotten what—enough![10]

The "enough" is a simple exclamatory fragment, scarcely worthy of being counted a syntactic variation. Similarly, the "O" followed by a repeated preposition constitutes a dislocation of very minor character, introduced to render the tone conversational and informal. Contrast these lines with Hopkins' pair of fragments "Sister, a sister calling/ A master, her master and mine!" which conveys considerable information in abbreviated form and knits it into a compact unit by means of repeated words and possessive pronouns. Despite their punctuation, the Hopkins fragments scarcely ring true as a spontaneous outcry. Very often Yeats departs from the traditional order of written English in order to capture the idiom of unmeditated speech. Hopkins, on the other hand, does not alter his style by accommodating it to slightly specialized dialects; his daring is far more than a matter of degree.

It appears that a charge of obscurity leveled against Yeats could hardly be based on what this study reveals about his method of putting words together. His high reputation would likewise seem to derive primarily from virtues other than the pattern of his language. Of course, the larger patterns that sentences make within stanzas, or stanzas within poems, may be responsible for aesthetic virtues or faults; but this question is too complicated to broach here and bears more especially on the following discussion of Eliot's poetry. Yeats, like Stevens, manifests greatest originality in his choice of words and in the unique values he discovers within them or manages to attach to them. He casts a thought, usually, in the molds at hand, increasing but little their flexibility. The long fragment beginning the third stanza of the third section of "The Tower," which John Unterecker records as an example of "strange syntax," would be remarkable in a Hopkins poem for its staidness.[11] The predominant conventionality of Yeats's sentences and his idiomatic fragmentation indicate that his style may be in part modeled on normal patterns of English speech. This is one recent manner in poetry.

The other significant departure from the style of most poets of the nineteenth century involves a thorough distortion or even destruction of traditional sentence patterns. The abnormal dislocations, complex fragments, and unique combinations of such deviations found in Hopkins foreshadow, and often crown, this development. Like Whitman, and like a number of French poets utterly foreign in spirit and method, Hopkins succeeded in making a language far more flexible, both as material for design and as a musical instrument, than its structure had before allowed. At the same time this flexibility seems to make for arduous reading. While, for some, freedom stimulates valuable invention; for others it brings hazards mitigating much of the advantage of license. Whatever judgment is passed on Hopkins' style and whatever the reasons for its composition, one cannot fail to see that the impulse to fabricate "original, spare and strange" sentences produces poetry of a special character and with special problems, while the plainspokenness of Yeats's work provides the model for another stylistic vein also with tone, effects, and limitations peculiar to itself.

BROWNING AND ELIOT

IN THE FIRST 500 LINES of Browning's longest narrative poem, *The Ring and the Book,* the poet relates how he found an old parchment-book, kernel of the story, in a market square in Florence. Gradually, he shifts the focus from himself, as engrossed browser, to the text, which thereafter forms the main substance of the poem. Yet throughout, Browning's style is the lens through which we see the plot develop. He muses, digresses, comments. At no point do we lose contact with the author's monologue, whereas the actors in the ancient drama continually fade and revive in our consciousness. In this poem, then, it is possible to assess the author's style in an extensive passage without too much troublesome interference from the dramatic *personae* which in so many other poems possess a certain autonomous value.

The syntax displayed in the beginning of the poem departs radically from the linguistic norm defined in the first chapter. Not only are there numerous examples of the fragmented forms and parenthetical disruptions often found in the spoken language, but also the reader is led into labyrinthine structures containing all of the major variations from standard syntax. Nearly one-half of the 195 discrete structures which occur in these 500 lines are to be classified as unusual. There is an especially high percentage of elaborate elements, many of them composed of three or four subordinate clauses in addition to the main one; and within these subordinate structures are other long chains of modifiers, many of them dislocated. By no stretch of the imagination could most of these elaborate constructions be considered as mere expansions of basically normal sentence skeletons; they are likewise much more intricate than colloquial patterns of speech.

These complex sentences resemble not a form of communication but a *form of imaginative perception*. That form occurs in the state of consciousness, peculiar to an individual at certain moments of his psychic life, when external reality and meditation interact in a confused mosaic of visual impressions, feelings, fantasies, and reflections. In this passage the individual is Browning, the environment Florence, and the principal object of attention the old book of court proceedings. All these elements are combined not in an orderly, discursive narrative, but in an apparently disjointed sequence of phrases. The narrative is sustained, and Browning shifts from regular conversational patterns to more discontinuous and elaborate forms and back again; but at many points the poet seems to be striving to render the very form and body of his thought, not simply to condense and prune it into the standard code of communication. One especially elaborate construction may serve to illustrate not only this dramatizing of mental life, but also the difficulty of analyzing Browning's syntax by means of conventional terminology:

This book—precisely on that palace step
Which, meant for lounging knaves o' the Medici,
Now serves re-venders to display their ware,—
'Mongst odds and ends of ravage, picture-frames
White through the worn gilt, mirror-sconces
    chipped,
Bronze angel-heads once knobs attached to chests
(Handled when ancient dames chose forth bro-
    cade),
Modern chalk drawings, studies from the nude,
Samples of stone, jet, breccia, porphyry
Polished and rough, sundry amazed busts
In baked earth (broken, Providence be praised!)
A wreck of tapestry, proudly-purposed web
When reds and blues were indeed red and blue,
Now offered as a mat to save bare feet
(Since carpets constitute a cruel cost)
Treading the chill scagliola bedward; then
A pile of brown-etched prints, two *crazie* each,
Stopped by a conch a-top from fluttering forth
—Sowing the Square with works of one and the
    same
Master, the imaginative Sienese
Great in the scenic backgrounds—(name and fame
None of you know, nor does he fare the worse:)
From these . . . Oh, with a Lionard going cheap
If it should prove, as promised, that Joconde

Whereof a copy contents the Louvre!—these
I picked this book from.

Note that this passage contains at least one exclamatory fragment "Oh, with a Lionard going cheap . . ." and a striking example of dislocation: the object—though there may be some difficulty in determining that it can be so classified—of the main verb, "This book," stands first in the sentence and is separated from the verb by two immense attributes themselves of a somewhat doubtful function. Even if we consider "This book," a reinforcing appositive phrase, it is certainly not apposite in any normal grammatical sense of the term. Even more remarkable, the primary elements of the sentence cannot be clearly integrated according to standard grammar. If we write the sentence skeleton this way, "This book . . . these I picked this book from," what can we call the reiteration "From these . . ." and what function shall we assign to the prepositional phrase beginning with " 'Mongst" and extending over 19 lines? Has this phrase been dislocated from a proper context ("From amongst these . . .")? If so we are still faced with an extra, nonparallel "from these." Or does the phrase modify the subject "I"? And what about the prior prepositional modifier, "precisely on that palace-step," which could be a complement of the subject or an adverbial element?

I suggest that no conventional grammatical analysis can resolve the ambiguities inherent in this construction. The dashes employed to separate items do not clearly signal grammatical relations, and we would be forced to stretch the meaning of "appositive phrase" out of all recognition in order to account for the position of "This book . . ." and "From these. . . ." Consequently, there are no standard traits of position or punctuation to give this passage syntactic unity.

Let us consider the passage in a different light. Besides the exclamatory fragment, four parenthetical asides interrupt the sequence of attributes linked to the preposition " 'Mongst." All of these represent strictly personal reflections of the author, brought on, it seems, when one of the objects in his field of imaginative vision generates a brief subjective response. The quick vision of the pile of prints whisked across the square, a vision purely imaginary, never realized because of the conch shell, also seems a gratuitous image projected on the scene by the poet. This mingling of observed detail, personal and selective response, and disruptive flashes of imagination—all framed by parts of a declarative sentence which ostensibly advances the narrative—indicates that the poet has organized his material partly according to principles other than the ordinary syntactic ones. The use of the dash and the series of dots, both of which represent sharp breaks in "thought" and do not clearly signal grammatical relationships, also suggests that the standard sentence mold has been deliberately broken. In addition, certain attributes, like the extra "From these," are "hovering" elements with an ambiguous or indeterminate grammatical function.

Despite the unorthodox construction of the "sentence," the meaning of it is clear enough. It is only doubtful that this clarity stems from the use of those conventional devices of language which insure certain communication. Rather, does not the poet lead us into a pattern roughly corresponding to the activity of the mind in relatively relaxed but intensely subjective states? Certainly the progression of the structure follows a darting, disorderly path: from the book, simply evoked by its name, our attention shifts abruptly to the whole panorama of its environment, and from thence to a purely imagined disruption of that environment, then to a half-ironic, half-wistful outburst over the Lionard, and finally to the narrative statement, which reintroduces the reader to the immediate subject of the poem. All this occurs between two periods.

Since 31 elaborate constructions appear in the total of 195 structures, and many of these also contain dislocated attributes, it is safe to say that Browning often built sentences of a special sort of complexity. The repeated use of dashes, dots, and parentheses as methods of linking dislocated and paratactic elements tells us that he preferred to rely on the most general and indeterminate of signals to relate these elements. Still, the poet employs some kind of typographical signal to mark these sudden shifts in the focus of attention; and though complex in a special way, his elaborate sentences have boundaries and subdivisions.

Also, some of the fragments have clear punctuation —question mark or exclamation point—which gives them an absolute grammatical value. These fragments would, in context, qualify as self-sufficient structures for many a scientific linguist. The intonation represented by the question mark in the sentence "Time for chow?" constitutes an "attribute" which conveys a complete and quite specific meaning as long as the context includes one speaker and at least one auditor. The autonomy of the exclamation "Some fun!" is likewise justified by its intonation and thus by its marking. Five fragments are patterned on these models.

In short, Browning exploits certain auxiliary devices of the language, devices almost more typographical than grammatical, in order to illustrate the activity of a mind at once keenly observing and imaginative. To an extent, the coercive power of language as a body of rules endowed with the sanction of tradition seems to have been denied. Instead the poet has attempted to distort the sentence mold in order to follow the nimble and intricate movements of his mind.

The poet often considered the principal exponent of a new manner in English poetry, T. S. Eliot, presents at first glance a syntactic physiognomy sharply different from that of Browning. The difference is in part one of quality. Again, certain passages are difficult to analyze in the terminology of classical grammar, but the problems are unlike Browning's troublesome repetitions and apostrophes.

Before exploring these qualitative differences we may mention that Eliot's career seems to have followed a pattern quite the reverse of Hopkins' and Yeats's. The syntax of the latter two poets grew more experimental as they matured. A glance at *Four Quartets,* Eliot's only poem of more than 500 lines, will convince the reader that the poet's later style nearly approaches the orthodoxy of prose, while the two earlier poems analyzed here, "Gerontion" and *The Waste Land,* contain much innovation. They employ lines of irregular length and erratic punctuation, as well as liberal quotations from both English and foreign languages. One would logically expect to find also greater variety of syntax here.

The small number of elaborate constructions indicates that Eliot's structures tend to be briefer than Browning's. This supposition is born out in the totals for the two samples. Eliot composed five discrete structures for every three of Browning's. At the same time, both the Eliot and Browning texts contain a large proportion of fragments. Clearly, however, Browning writes longer and more elaborate sentences than does Eliot. The latter's style appears to be an odd combination of choppy, colloquial sentences of standard pattern with a liberal share of fragments.

When one examines these fragments more closely, the unusualness of Eliot's style becomes immediately apparent. Many of Browning's sentences contained dislocations which could be so identified because the ultimate boundaries of the construction (the beginning capital and terminating period) and the internal separating and connecting signals (commas, dashes, dots) forced the reader to reorganize sentence elements included within the boundaries into a grammatical pattern. Similarly, fragments were recognized as discrete

structures because they too were bounded by typographical signals. In a few the exclamation or question
mark sufficed to complete the meaning of the element
and form a kind of independent "sentence."

Very often these signals are entirely lacking for
Eliot, and whether one word group belongs with another or is distinct from it cannot be determined for
certain. In some cases it is impossible to know whether
the poet has dislocated a phrase and means it to be
reintegrated into a larger structure or has simply juxtaposed two discrete elements without signaling their
boundaries. The recurrence of this problem suggests
that such ambiguity is intentional.

Consider the following excerpt from "The Fire Ser-
mon":

> Elizabeth and Leicester
> Beating oars
> The stern was formed
> A gilded shell
> Red and Gold
> The brisk swell
> Rippled both shores
> Southwest wind
> Carried down stream
> The peal of bells
> White towers
> > Weialala leia
> > Wallala leialala
> > "Trams and dusty trees.
> Highbury bore me. Richmond and Kew
> Undid me. By Richmond I raised my knees
> Supine on the floor of a narrow canoe."

* * * * * * * * * * * * * * * * * * *

> "On Margate Sands.
> I can connect
> Nothing with nothing.

The broken fingernails of dirty hands.
My people humble people who expect
Nothing."
   la la
To Carthage then I came
   Burning burning burning burning
O Lord Thou pluckest me out
O Lord thou pluckest
burning

Obviously we cannot begin with the first line of this passage and proceed to the first period in order to establish the boundaries of a sentence. Even the first four lines cannot be related by means of traditional grammar and conventions of punctuation. What is the relation between "Elizabeth and Leicester" and "Beating oars"? If we term them fragments instead of a fused structure or dislocated elements, we are forced to do so on semantic grounds; for there is no physical property other than the uncertain independence of the poetic line to determine how or to what degree the words are differentiated. Similarly ambiguous is the function of "White towers" or "Burning." Here not even meaning is much help. On the other hand, some elements, like "The broken fingernails of dirty hands," occur between recognizable signals which set them off as discrete structures. But with or without boundary signals, the relation of these structures to their context must be determined semantically. Signals seem to occur, then, somewhat arbitrarily; here their distribution is especially remarkable.

In place of the extensive use of dashes, dots, and parentheses, Eliot substitutes the break of the poetic line and the disposition of lines on the page as a syntactic principle. A more indeterminate and ungrammatical set of signals can hardly be imagined. If, by exploiting the most flexible of syntactic devices, Browning strained customary sentence molds to the breaking point, in Eliot the molds have burst. Browning's digression from book to piazza to Italian history and back to book is always connected, though often very tenuously, by means of the author's unifying consciousness as he observes, meditates, peruses the story. The threads of digressive thought are not all loose ends; they are continually brought back to the subject at hand, the book. In the cited passage we see this divagation and return crammed into the framework of a single sentence.

Not so with Eliot. Many of his structures have no convenient divisions, and the mixture of dialogue, literary allusion, parody, and flat statement hardly sketches a state of consciousness, unless it be a highly idiosyncratic one. A great many of the fragments in the Eliot passage simply evoke an image which neither by its punctuation and position nor by its ostensible meaning can be syntactically related to adjoining words. All of Browning's fragmentary structures seem to be either accompanied by an attribute of intonation (?, !), or associated with a verb as nominative absolutes, constructions modeled on the grammatical, Latin ablative absolute. This association is always traced by a typographical signal: colon, comma, or dash. But Eliot's phrase "The broken fingernails of dirty hands," and the unattached and unbounded elements "Burning burning burning," appear to float between or near other elements which exert a nearly equal attraction on them. The phrases and their contexts can, indeed, be considered a kind of "fused" structure. Can we be sure whether the Lord is burning or Carthage, the "I" or the atmosphere out of which the "I" is being plucked? Are broken fingernails an illustration of the difficulty of connecting things or a picturesque detail of the appearance of "humble people"? These ambiguities cannot be resolved by syntactic analysis nor, probably, are they meant to be.

Two of the consequences, then, of Eliot's use of linebreak and the disposition of lines as syntactic devices, are the sharper dissociation of paratactic elements and ambiguity stemming from the fusion of structures. Whether or not these devices represent an attempt to reflect a dynamic state of consciousness, a psychic personality, they do constitute a radical extension of earlier methods which attempted to accomplish that task. If, indeed, Eliot has in any way sought to build a model of a mentality, the blank space between lines and the failure to provide unambiguous signals may represent the obscure transformation of one thought or image into another, or the abrupt flash of an apparently irrelevant image in the midst of a train of connected mental events. Browning accomplishes this end mostly within the framework of traditional grammar, but Eliot is obviously striving at certain points to communicate according to principles quite other than those of traditional linguistic patterns. As a preliminary to the formulation of these principles, one may state that they must account for these facts: poetry in the style of Eliot contains sentences briefer and simpler than the conventionally elaborated structures of earlier poets; this poetry also dispenses with many of the signals, grammatical and typographic, which mark relationships in ordinary written communication; and the large number of hovering elements and fused structures suggests that radical dissociation and ambiguity of sentence elements are inherent in this style.

In the poetry of Yeats and Eliot, then, we find the dominant syntactic characteristics of much modern poetry, and in selections from Hopkins and Browning we discover early examples of experimentation with these structures. Hopkins, it appears, has a set of distinctive syntactic idiosyncrasies, yet these extraordinary structures have certain formal properties in common with poetry written after 1920 (the "hovering" element). Yeats does not experiment much with sentence structure, and this regularity can be cited as another dominant mode in twentieth-century verse. In Browning's work, large numbers of fragments combine with other variations to produce special effects on the reader. Browning, like Hopkins, may create an elaborate sentence containing multiple dislocations, especially interrupting fragments, but his aim is akin to Yeats's—to simulate in written form the spoken language. Yeats's speech is simply the tidier and more declamatory. Eliot appears to have sought to achieve, by means of a mingling of regular sentences and highly independent fragments, somewhat different ends, which involve the rejection not only of conventions of written English but also sometimes of the common patterns of coherent speech.

All these poets, except Yeats, owe their reputations for difficulty or obscurity in part to an unorthodox syntax. These two terms are of course not interchangeable. The poetry of Hopkins or Browning may force a reader to concentrate heavily; but most of their lines, however contorted, can be comprehended and related one to another by means of explicit grammatical signals: verb endings, relative pronouns, proximity of modifier to modified, and punctuation. Still, a large number of variations seems to make immediate comprehension difficult. In Yeats, however, there are sentences of perfectly ordinary structure, yet of uncertain meaning— like "I would be ignorant as the dawn"—so that the reader must admit the preeminent role of the semantic content of words in communicating thought. When a poet relies solely upon this semantic element, as Eliot often does, by eliminating the customary devices by which even fragments are given some relation to their context, his work may indeed become obscure to those who are accustomed to define a word by its use in a sentence, rather than by its use in a whole poem.

The structure of these poets' sentences is neither pure convention nor gratuitous decoration, but an integral element in the meaning and emotional effect of their poetry. Ideally, structure acts in harmony with vocabulary to create an aesthetic experience. Therefore, when poetic style changes between two periods or when poets habitually use the same structure in similar ways, it is proper to view these changes and affinities not as mere historical oddities but as signs of different or similar assumptions about the nature and function of poetry. In the following chapter I consider two possible consequences of viewing syntax as an expression of such assumptions: Since both the poet and his language are in part products of time and place, it is possible that the change in poetic style between 1870 and 1930 is related to changes in the social and intellectual climate in which the poetry was produced. Then, too, a change in style due to a new conception of the poetic resources of language may require a new approach to individual poems; to read modern poetry profitably, we may have to take into account its unusual structures as the means to unusual ends.

5

The Context of the Change

PEOPLE'S SPEECH

WHEN THE ELABORATE sentences of Victorian poets give
way to the broken bits and spare utterances of the
Imagistes, and when the monotonous, ritualized inversions of traditional English poetry are discarded in
favor of plain speech or, occasionally, a wildly scram-
bled word order, these obvious contrasts conceal some
subtler distinctions and connections. In the excessive
elaborations found in late nineteenth-century poetry,
nouns gain "centrifugal force" until they become nearly
independent units, foreshadowing later fragments built
on a noun kernel; the exclamatory fragment found in
traditional verse has little in common with phlegmatic
fragments written by poets of the early twentieth century; Longfellow's dislocations, likewise, differ markedly from Cummings'; and the elaborateness of Victorian poetry, a swelling by means of subordinate
clauses, does not resemble the "cataloguing" popular
among Whitman's successors. Finally, we may note
something of a paradox. The poets of the first quarter
of this century write mostly in two modes, apparently
opposed: they break violently the traditional molds of
the language by leaving out grammatical elements
essential to the formation of sentences, or they adhere
rather closely to the most common patterns by which
sentences are formed. Sometimes, the two tendencies

are manifest in the same writer, as in Williams, Stevens, and Lawrence.

The stylistic change charted here was partly the conscious revolt of a new generation of poets against the mannerisms of some of their predecessors. Yet the rebels did not seek an entirely original style; they adapted somewhat to models readily on hand in their own and in foreign literatures. Thus Pound and Eliot looked to France and the Orient. What they learned there, to be sure, they shaped to suit their own purposes; but to understand why English-speaking poets sought to capture stylistic effects cultivated in French and Japanese, we must ask what those effects are.

Before 1870, few English poets troubled themselves about contemporary foreign literature.[1] Tennyson and Browning, for the most part, ignored Hugo and Baudelaire. Arnold paid respectful but not very close attention to his continental contemporaries. Swinburne and Wilde were among the first to esteem highly the French poetry of their day; and Swinburne, especially, recognized in Gautier and Baudelaire kindred spirits.[2] However, one must avoid confusing the subject matter of an archetypal Symbolist poet like Baudelaire—Swinburne and Pound would jointly praise the bile, sensuality, egocentricity of the Frenchman—and the form of his language, which Swinburne sometimes approximates and to which Pound offers a sharp contrast. For Pound, certainly, attempts to break with the Swinburnian style.

Taupin in his thorough account of the French influence on American poetry during the crucial decade 1910–1920, asserts that Marianne Moore, Wallace Stevens, William Carlos Williams, Hart Crane and E. E. Cummings, as well as Pound and Eliot, all owe much to the French tradition.[3] He claims that even those like Crane, who had no mastery of tongues and knew French poets only casually, were touched by that tradition. Only in general terms, however, does he discuss this powerful and pervasive influence. More specific evidence for the debt is not far to seek.

From Rémy de Gourmont, critic and poet; from Mallarmé, Jammes, Fort, Verhaeren, Régnier and Viélé-Griffin; from Laforgue and Corbière, the little band of poets known as Imagistes drew a brief catalogue of poetic principles.[4] This credo, very roughly, was simply to use as little and as definite language as possible to convey precise feelings. Fragments thus became not merely acceptable but desirable.[5] It was only necessary that they be *concrete*, as Hulme is forever insisting. A poem widely admired by the Imagistes, de Gourmont's *Litanies de la Rose,* is made up almost entirely of fragments.[6] They occur also in Rimbaud's "Voyelles," "Mémoire," and "Bruxelles"; in Mallarmé's "Salut"; in Verhaeren's "La Mort" and "La Recherche"; and in occasional poems of Viélé-Griffin, like "Le Gue" and "Par la Roseraie." The image, naked and alone, became a mode of expression, and the noun, of course, its principal element.

From the turn of the century on, avant-garde French poetry and the most modern verse in English ran a parallel course. To trace and weigh mutual influence and counterinfluence during this period, when a dozen major poets crossed paths in nearly as many countries— writing to, about, and for or against one another in two or three languages—would require a careful book, of which now, one can only tick off a few chapter headings: punctuation—it disappears at about the same time in the work of Apollinaire and Eliot, Pound and Williams; prose-poetry—it appears in Amy Lowell and in Max Jacob, though Rimbaud had already done such verse in *Une Saison en enfer;* predecessors—while Pound was discovering the new French poets some of those very same poets were discovering Whitman,[7] the only major poet included in this study who spews fragments in quantities worthy of Pound himself; common influences—the Imagistes became interested in Oriental verse forms just as, earlier, Jammes and Fort had; [8] popular idiom—scraps from newspapers, street songs, idle conversation crop up in Apollinaire and Cocteau just as Eliot, Pound, Sandburg, and Williams experiment with the same sources.[9]

The list could be greatly extended. Here we need only note that certain syntactic peculiarities in twentieth-century English and American poetry—especially fragmentation and its attendant ambiguity—have analogues in French poetry. An attempt to make precise the nature of this correlation would end in confusion, I suspect. One school of French poets, from Mallarmé through Claudel and Valéry, tried to develop a mandarin dialect, poetry of a syntax subtle and intricate, but not irreparably shattered.[10] Only very indirectly is this school related to the poetry in English of this century, characterized as it is by that odd ambivalence: free, discrete fragments and the plain patterns of everyday speech. Taupin pinpoints the difference in contrasting the obscurity of Mallarmé with that of H.D.: the links in the Frenchman's structures are unorthodox, rarefied; between the English poet's images, often, no links exist.[11] Still more confusing, another branch of French poetry, beginning with Rimbaud and surviving in Apollinaire, the Surrealist Breton, and eventually Jacques Prévert, has obvious stylistic similarities to many contemporary English and American poets—disintegrating sentences, catalogues, colloquial if not slang structures—yet the foremost members of the two groups seem largely indifferent to if not ignorant of one another. Finally, critics mention the Mallarméan "symbolist" tradition as a significant influence on English and American poetry, while cubist and surrealist poets are supposed to have affected our verse forms hardly at all.[12]

Probably, as in many such puzzles, everyone is right. In the first place, the avant-garde English and American poets of the 1920s and 1930s did not pattern their work closely after any single foreign artist or school. They absorbed general *tones*—cynicism, irony, allusiveness— from some poets, general principles of style—a taste for concrete diction, elipsis, daring line disposition— from others. They sometimes misunderstood their idols, doubtless. In any event, what similarities in syntax we discover between French, and English and American poetry would probably not be best explained as examples of the direct impact of some writers on others.

Even if such an impact could be proved, more profound questions remain. What attracted English-speaking poets to these experiments in another language? Did the French supply not only powder and shot but also the intellectual spark for a full-scale revolution in English prosody? Further, why should such a radical break with tradition be so widely, so enthusiastically, so quickly hailed? (Fletcher compared the discovery of free verse with the discovery of radium; [13] Shapiro claims that the new forms of the Imagistes constitute one of English poetry's "few great upheavals," a "first major mutation since the time of Chaucer" in prosody.[14]) To answer such questions, one must look not for superficial "influences," but for the pervasive forces that mold the intellectual life of large communities, international communities, making them responsive to certain dominant art forms, fashions, and systems of government or economy.

It is probably apparent by now that this study concerns itself with the rise of "modern" poetry more than with the decline of traditional verse. The problem, then, is to understand why fragmentation, extremely radical dislocation, and the patterns of common speech become of use to poets. One immediate objection to this phrasing of the matter would occur to those who have had some training in historical linguistics. Perhaps the tendency toward regularity noticeable in some twentieth-century poetry only reflects a similar tendency in the gradual mutation of the whole language.

"Thus," states Jespersen, "order and consistency signalize the modern stage of the English language." [15] And one of the two major drifts in the structuring of this language, says Sapir, is "the tendency to fixed position in the sentence, determined by the syntactic relation of the word." [16] Does Frost invert sentences rarely, then, because the character of the language restrains him from doing so? To some degree, perhaps, word order may have become more rigid during the 60-year span here surveyed, but the change could hardly be so violent as that charted for the poetry of the period. It is much more likely that poetry like Longfellow's or Morris' never had much affinity with the language as it was spoken, while that of Dickinson, Emerson, and Hardy did; and that Frost chose to write as he did knowing full well that his words would fall into well-worn grooves. Certainly he saw the value of "everyday talk" for poetry: "The common speech is always giving off, you and I know how, the special vocabulary of poetry. The same thing happens with the tones of everyday talk. They have emanations of grandeur and dignity and reverence and heroism and terror." [17] And for such preferences, of course, he drew praise,[18] and that reaction interests us.

In earlier chapters we have seen that Yeats, Hopkins, and Pound esteemed poetry of a colloquial form or pace. Yeats apparently grew aware of his taste for colloquial structure only gradually; he wrote to H. J. C. Grierson in 1926, "My own verse has more and more adopted—seemingly without any will of mine—the syntax and vocabulary of common personal speech." [19] Bits of transcribed talk, we have noted, appear in Eliot, Crane, and Auden. Williams, more daring than Wordsworth, thus endorses with much sanction not poetry *like* the speech of common men, but speech *as* poetry.

It is nothing of a poet's business to be a critic of his own work. Critical processes must take place in him but they need very careful watching lest they upset something far more important in him, his sensibility to the *speech* about him and its meaning, its pace, its form.

* * * * * * *

I, too, am looking for what he [Yvor Winters] is looking for but I am looking for it in the *speech* about me. I am trying to see how far I can fit that speech to a formal pattern. I am trying to combine substance and form which, by the way, is the problem of the artist pure and simple, to give the form significance.[20]

A comparison of the vocabulary and the syntax of any of these poets would reveal that their poetry mimics common speech in form, not content. Words like "sussurus" or "Brueghel" do not appear often in everyday speech; subjects before verbs do.

Jespersen seems to misunderstand the poetry of his own time when he says,

On the whole, however, modern poets do not take their grammar from any one old author or book, but are apt to use any deviation from the ordinary grammar they can lay hold of anywhere. And thus it has come to pass in the nineteenth century that while the languages of other civilized nations have the same grammar for poetry as for prose, although retaining here and there a few archaic forms of verbs, etc., in English a wide gulf separates the grammar of poetry from that of ordinary life.[21]

As the table in Appendix I clearly shows, however, one of the variations of modern poetry—even in the nineteenth century—was *toward* ordinary structures, and subsequent work has only reinforced that drift, narrowing the "wide gulf" between literature and normal speech. It is true that the drift to colloquialism is only one current in twentieth-century poetry, but it is a strong and a steady current, as noticeable, if not as striking, as that of fragmentation.

What pressures could have made the patterns of common speech a poetic virtue? One correlation immediately presents itself. From the French Revolution to the Russian Revolution of 1917, a period of a little more than a century, Europe, England, and America were swept by democratic or popular movements for reform. In French schools, for example, shortly after the revolution, the intensive study of Latin and classic literature gave way to the reading of Shakespeare and Ossian. The cultured, the literate, the noble were deprived of privilege in the course of these reforms, and the peasant, the laborer, the backwoodsman rose to some degree of power and influence. And to celebrate the common man become king, Lincoln, came the popular journalist become poet, Whitman. Some literary embellishments understandably fell from favor in the process.

The apotheosis of the common man may have affected the composition of poetry irrespective of the political affiliations of poets. Of course, in some instances men of limited education and no profound knowledge of the traditional flourishes of English verse became widely appreciated men of letters. Whitman, Stephen Crane, Twain, and Hemingway first wrote for newspapers—the popular press being the literary expression of the new power of Everyman.[22] But even poets like Pound and Eliot, whose *odi profanum* feelings are no secret, express themselves more as Sweeney speaks than as Milton writes. In his letters, for example, Pound manifests an almost obsessive tendency to slide into a transcription of semiliterate dialect. *Wuz* appears nearly as often as *was* in some letters. *Aints* abound. Irony, of course, is intended; but in some of the late cantos the same habits recur monotonously long after the force of the irony has been worn away.

114

When dia   significant
movement i   w and Luv-
ingood, it is   rous irony.
Cultured me   guistic slum-
ming. But i   e colloquial
bent, as in I   le natural to
the art. Son   n." [23] But all
might agree   ctations, becoming stru   t was otherwise used, c   this century.
And it is n   at this revolution in sty   nmon speech
become a]   in some way
to social a   ein the com-
mon man achieves suffrage, educationai prerogatives,
and moral authority.

Some may heatedly oppose this conclusion, reflect-
ing that poets for nearly a half-century have been accused of writing for a very small coterie of readers,
those especially attuned to new, subtle idioms. The ac-
cusation is not without foundation: Eliot's allusions
baffle all but the most literary at first; Graves expects a
knowledge of mythology; Crane puzzled his early re-
viewers; few men have mastered the Cantos; and
Thomas and Cummings can be impermeable. How,
then, can one suggest that the structure of poetic language has anything at all to do with the rise of a culture geared to the needs of "the people"? If most people do not comprehend them, surely these writers do
not speak *plainly*. Yet they often do. Whether or not
we understand what the poets "say," of course, is another matter.

It is obvious that some writers, like Frost and Sandburg, have considerable popular appeal. And these two,
admittedly, cultivate an off-hand colloquialism. It is
true also that the more notoriously obscure poets are
capable of constructing sentences which no one is likely
ever to hear in casual conversation. But typographical

experiments and intermittent fragmentation aside, even the most difficult modern poetry usually approximates, in form, everyday speech. An examination of the first lines of *The Waste Land* or *The Man with the Blue Guitar* suffices to prove the point.

Here again we may profit by a glance at the recent history of French literature. The tradition of the popular lyric in France is an old one, and that tradition nourished some of those poets—Laforgue, Corbière, Apollinaire—who most influenced experimental verse in France, Britain, and America.[24] Elizabeth Drew claims that American poets picked up, from this dissonant minor in the symbolist concert, their taste for turns of common speech.[25] From Gallic song to *The Waste Land* may appear to be an impossible leap, yet in France there developed an even more confusing disparity between manner and matter, forerunner and disciple. The surrealist poets, descendants of Apollinaire, who himself is not remarkable for simplicity, allied themselves with the Communist party. Breton, Aragon, and later Prévert managed to combine proletarian sympathies and the most radical experimentation with language. The experimentation, nevertheless, contained broad streaks of flat statement and vulgar diction. Ezra Pound the Fascist expatriate, Wallace Stevens the insurance executive, and André Breton the revolutionary—a bizarre group to be sure—thus share a literary heritage and perhaps illustrate the diffuse but penetrating power of cultural change.

> I make a pact with you Walt Whitman
> I have detested you long enough.
> I come to you as a grown child
> Who has had a pig-headed father;
> I am old enough now to make friends.[26]

> Among twenty snowy mountains
> the only moving thing

Was the eye of a blackbird.
I was of three minds,
Like a tree
In which there are three blackbirds.[27]

Je ne suis pas pour les adeptes
Je n'ai jamais habité au lieudit la Grenouillère
La lampe de mon coeur file et bientôt hoquète à
    l'approcho doo parvio
Je n'ai jamais été porté que vers ce qui ne se tenait
    pas à carreau [28]

In all these poems, the sentences are perfectly regular,
as one would speak them. Subjects precede verbs; dependent clauses are few and uncomplicated. Had we
objectivity enough, the similarity of such excerpts
would strike us as forcefully as that in a selection of
couplets from Boileau, Pope, and Barlow.

Pound's political sympathies and his affected esoter-
ism should not forbid our crediting him with a sus-
ceptibility to the form and pressure of the time. If
he taught his successors "an awareness of verse as
speech," [29] he only demonstrates how unerring and un-
shakeable was his instinct for forwarding the development of his art, however bitter his opposition to the
age in which that art was imbedded. Eliot and Stevens,
otherwise so different, manifest this awareness just as
surely. Cummings has tried his hand at straight talk;

it started when Bill's chip let on to
the bulls he'd bumped a bloke back in fifteen.
Then she came toward him on her knees across the
    locked
    room. he knocked her cold and beat it for Chi-
    cago.[30]

It is commonplace to note the colloquialism of Sandburg.[31] More surprising is Louise Bogan's claim that

117

E. A. Robinson based his idiom "squarely on the everyday New England speech of his period." [32] One may omit the "squarely" and yet marvel that a poet born before Bryant died, an arch-conservative compared to Frost, could still be counted among those who speak naturally. Certainly, the obvious symptoms of a literature affected somehow by the masses—neo-Marxist ideas in some poets and pungent slang in others—are less impressive as evidence of a stylistic revolution than this set of pervasive syntactic traits, which embraces so many major poets of diverse persuasion.

It is not a question of simple causal relation; a complete account of the subtle and multiple links between a literature and its society defies human understanding. But we would expect, in the century of universal suffrage, the popular press, public education, and immense technical extensions of the power of speech—phonograph, telephone, wireless—that poetry would undergo changes, be somehow marked. It does indeed bear a mark: whatever difficulties his vocabulary offers and however intricate the overall structure of his work may be, in a good many of his moods a modern poet, taken line by line, talks to us.

FRAGMENTS: THE MIND MIRRORS ITSELF ANEW

"To cut the cackle—that was to be the first aim of a modern poetry." [33] Sir Herbert Read's reference to the literary revolt of his generation suggests a relation between the poetry of plain talk and the clusters of fragments which so often interrupt it. There are two ways to cut the cackle. One may turn it into straightforward parlance; or one may remove all but a few suggestive words. The distribution of syntactic variations among the poets of the 1930 group indicates, in fact, that both methods are in operation simultaneously and that both lead away from the dominant style of the Victorian age.

Yet, again, these tendencies appear contradictory. Simplification of structure ought to make poetry easier to grasp. Omission could well make it harder. Perhaps, indeed, such a difference would explain why modern poets, despite their evident colloquial mannerism, are still accused of obscurity. When they talk, we understand; when they begin stuttering in fragments, the reader cannot follow. This explanation, appealing in its simplicity, would fail to fit the facts.

For example, a good many extremely simple, extremely regular sentences do not yield their meaning readily, "The sea," writes Stevens, "is a form of ridicule." Or, again, "Morning is not sun,/ It is this posture of the nerves. . . ." [34] One of this poet's favorite devices consists of linking by a copula two concepts of striking dissimilarity. The spark of comprehension may never bridge the gap left by the neutral "is," and if it does, the structure of the sentence will hardly be responsible. The nouns in both these "simple" statements emanate nuances which interact and deliver a charge of meaning and emotion—almost despite the routine pattern in which the nouns are cast. Another poet, an Imagiste perhaps, might have written

> The sea
> —a form of ridicule.
> Morning
> not sun
> but this posture of the nerves.

and a reader of moderate ingenuity would have understood the lines as readily as if linkage had been supplied.

On the other hand, not all fragments puzzle us. Consider a few lines from D. H. Lawrence's poem "The Fish":

Himself all silvery himself
In the element,
No more.
Nothing more.
Himself,
And the element.
Food, of course!
Water-eager eyes,
Mouth-gate open
And strong spine urging, driving;
And desirous belly gulping.[35]

Surely no one would argue that expanding these fragments into sentences ("All silvery in the elements, he
was himself and no more") would greatly clarify this
passage, or make it more accessible to a reader than it
already is. Stevens with verbs still puzzles us more than
Lawrence without them, so that whatever our com-
plaints against modern poetry, its faults, particularly
its "difficulty" or "obscurity," cannot be reduced to a
simple list of broken grammatical conventions.

Earlier, it was suggested that in one poet, Browning,
and in one genre, the dramatic monologue, the apparently contradictory tendencies of modern poetry were
harmonized. More or less ordered ruminations, passionate and explosive utterance, and inchoate thought before utterance—these formed the span of consciousness
this poet elected to represent as directly as his medium
permitted. Given such a range, the regular patterns of
English and dissociated parts of these patterns could
occur side by side—or, often, one within the other.

On the other hand, in a very different kind of poet,
Whitman, we observe a similar phenomenon: here are
great heaps of fragments, which not seldom grow out
of or melt into a series of sentences whose word order
is regular. Although the fact of fragmentation itself
relates them, the two poets use fragments in distinctly
different ways. A review of the selections from Brown-

ing in chapter 4 and from Whitman in chapter 3 convinces one of the distinction; for in a Browning poem, shreds of unrealized sentences may interrupt a speaker often, but not for long, giving the reader a reasonably accurate facsimile of consciousness just over and sometimes at the threshold of speech; but Whitman's catalogues no man would be likely to utter either aloud or to himself. There is also a rich multiplicity of subject matter in these catalogues that the stricter form of the dramatic monologue does not allow. For the moment, let us dwell on the essential quality of these two kinds of verse in turn.

Apparently the so-called dramatic monologue did not originate with Browning, since Fuson finds examples of the technique in Catullus, in early Anglo-Saxon literature, in Skelton, More, Daniel, Drayton, the Cavalier poets, and even in Pope.[36] Still, it is worth remembering that "In the half-century before Browning more monologs were turned out than were written during the five centuries before Blake and Burns," and that Browning "certainly dominated the field in the mid-nineteenth century and has influenced virtually all later developments in its artistry."[37] Not a lone genius, but one cresting a wave, Browning managed to purge the form of a certain taint of artificiality. He achieved an extraordinary degree of what Fuson calls "oral realism," as well as the other indispensable qualities of the form, "objectivity and internal drama."[38]

To this objectivity and oral realism later poets have given an unusual twist.

A final trend, the most provocative and sophisticated area of development in the genre since Browning, is that of the "interior monolog." This applies to the dense-textured, sometimes obscure, ironic, tortured, semi-oral semisubconscious maunderings of an "I" who is not primarily engaged in communication to an auditor but is preoccupied with his own subliminal spiritual crises. . . . A parallel development in prose is stream-of-consciousness technique, seen in Proust, Dujardin, Dorothy Richardson, and James Joyce.[39]

The colloquialism of poetry and of the novel in the twentieth century has already hinted at such a parallel. If dialogue has become a convenient mode of dramatizing external conflicts, surely some sort of imitation of inner verbalizing is necessary to portray the silent struggles of the soul. One would expect, if the parallel indeed holds, to find fragments in a novel like *Ulysses*. It is hardly necessary to go beyond the first page or two of the book to confirm this expectation.

We can now recall an interesting sequence of events. It appears that a kind of poetry long known but little exploited suddenly developed, in the latter half of the nineteenth century and at the hands of a master, great power and flexibility; and that poets in the next century extended the range of that power to achieve not only oral realism but psychic realism. Simultaneously, certain stylistic characteristics associated with this kind of poetry—the word order of everyday speech and frequent fragmentation—become dominant. One concludes that probably these devices of style are employed to convey the substance and movement of the mind, usually of a particular mind. Because the increase in the number of fragments in modern poetry is much sharper and more widespread than the slight rise in the number of regular structures, it is natural to suspect that the change in emphasis from oral to psychic realism brings with it a final reduction of muttered sentences, already stripped of their traces of flourish and elaboration, to mere parts of sentences.[40] If this speculation is sound, the cackle has been cut drastically indeed.

Just how the dramatic monologue became an interior monologue would be difficult to determine, but the step from expressed to unexpressed would seem a logical extension of the technique, designed as it was to reveal the inmost and often illicit desires of men and women. To a degree, however, the connection of this form with consciously verbalized feeling, with spoken language, inhibited its development as an instrument for plumbing deeper levels of the consciousness. Some early examples of the partly interior monologue, like "Prufrock" and *Mauberley*, are incontestably fine portraits of personalities; but they do not, except by implication, expose more than the surface play of a consciousness.

For example, Taupin, speaking of ellipsis in Pound and the other Imagistes, equates poem with thought, and implies thereby that a break in the structure of a stanza, line, or sentence should exactly express some lacuna in the development of a thought: "C'est dire que le poème est la pensée même, que toute modification de la forme serait une modification de la pensée. . . . Le poème est un état d'âme, et cet état d'âme donne au poème sa longeur, sa forme, dessine ses lignes droites, courbées, ou brisées. . . . Le poème peut être une rêverie qui se prolonge et se brise parfois par des visions claires, par des images précises." [41] According to such a view, the poem's organic unity is in part achieved by allowing for considerable disunity—fragmentation and dislocation by interruption, whenever such variations betray a characteristic mode of thought.

Again the course of French poetry provides a parallel. Marcel Raymond finds in Apollinaire's *Zone* "heterogeneous elements, sensations, judgments, memories intermingled just as in the flux of psychological life." [42] And speaking of later, even more exotic mingling, he notes that "this undisciplined use of language . . . has also been likened to the free and incoherent monologs that psychoanalysts try to obtain from their patients." [43] Such remarks remind one of similar ones made about poets in English, as when Edmund Wilson suggests that

Eliot has found for his complex subjects "a different language" and quotes May Sinclair, "His thoughts move very rapidly and by astounding cuts. They move not by logical stages and majestic roundings of the full literary curve, but as live thoughts move in live brains." [44] It is difficult, however, to imagine "unconscious thought" or to suggest how such thought might be represented on a page.

Inevitably, then, poetry deriving solely from the interior monologue preserves a connection with formulated, if not uttered, speech; it may contain interrupted sentences, frequent but intermittent fragments often obliquely related to the sense of the context, but will probably not overwhelm the reader with dense catalogues. Similarly, since a sentence can theoretically be broken off at any point, almost any sort of grammatical element—verb, adjective, adverb phrase as well as noun—may appear in a monologue dissociated from any sentence structure; but, of course, nouns or noun phrases as "descriptive" fragments make up most catalogues.

If, then, the style of Browning's monologues has been refined to penetrate into the twilight zones of consciousness, but no further, what of Whitman's heaps of nouns and exploding sentences? Perhaps the difference between the two poets has here been exaggerated. Their contemporaries were evidently struck by a certain likeness. "Professor Corson, the Browning scholar, wrote to Walt Whitman that he believed that impassioned Prose would be the medium in which the poetry of the future would be written, and that he considered the *Leaves of Grass* one of the harbingers. The vogue of free verse, which is but impassioned prose, shows that his prophesy is coming true." [45] "Whitman," the critic later observes, "is without a doubt the father of free verse in America and England today." [46] And *vers libre*, as Taupin, Lowes, Raymond, Shapiro, and others quoted earlier have demonstrated, was also, like the dramatic monologue, a movement toward the rhythm and word order of ordinary speech.

It would be a mistake, however, to stop at this superficial parallel. Whitman aimed at much more subtle and exotic effects than the cadence of common discourse alone. The linguist Edward Sapir, a critic oddly enough hostile to the revolution in verse forms, sensed a deeper accord between the two nineteenth-century forerunners of free verse and psychic realism:

> The artist's "intuition," to use Croce's term, is immediately fashioned out of a generalized human experience—thought and feeling—of which his own individual experience is a highly personalized selection. The thought relations in this deeper level have no specific linguistic vesture; the rhythms are free, not bound, in the first instance, to the traditional rhythms of the artist's language. Certain artists whose spirit moves largely in the non-linguistic (better, in the generalized linguistic) layer even find a certain difficulty in getting themselves expressed in the rigidly set terms of their accepted idiom. One feels that they are unconsciously striving for a generalized art language. . . . Their art expression is frequently strained, it sounds at times like a translation from an unknown original—which, indeed, is precisely what it is. These artists—Whitmans and Brownings—impress us rather by the greatness of their spirit than the felicity of their art.[47]

The terms "unconsciously striving" and "translation from an unknown original" are striking. Clearly, Sapir implies that both Browning and Whitman attempt to express the nonlinguistic, the "thought relation" having no linguistic "vesture," with words, and that they understandably fail. There is a strong suggestion here that by intuition operating at a deeper level is meant access to the subconscious. As we shall soon see, later poets certainly strove to draw material from the subconscious and transmit it more or less directly to the reader. And, indeed, if Browning foreshadowed the step from expressed to unexpressed thought, Whitman may have suggested a further step—from unexpressed to inexpressible.

Freud drew on Goethe and Schiller to prove the power of the unconscious in literary creation.[48] Quoting particularly the romantics—Shelley, Keats, Emerson, Poe, Wordsworth—Prescott suggests that poets have always been intrigued by dreams, betraying their instinctive grasp of the poetic worth of hidden mental resources. He refers triumphantly to Chabaneix's statement in *Le Subconscient:* "the participation of the unconscious in inspired creation is recognized by all who have approached the subject." [49] Mordell bases an even stronger series of claims on the literature of dreams. After mentioning dreams in Moses Ibn Ezra, Coleridge, Daudet, Emerson, Lowell, Poe, and Hearn, he states, "At all times, again, it was vaguely understood that dreams reveal the unconscious, that poetry emanates from the dream state," [50] adding later, "Poetry is the voice then of the unconscious. The poem is usually a product of the day-dream, which is related to the dream of sleep, for both species of dreams reveal the unconscious." [51] One may balk at forcing "The Vanity of Human Wishes" or "Essay on Criticism" to conform to such a definition of poetry, but these comments are useful as an indication of how thoroughly many literary men had committed themselves to new theories of the mind.

Though often unaware of its bias, modern poetry, according to certain other critics, most notably Wyndham Lewis in *Time and Western Man,* owes much to pervasive Bergsonian notions of psychic reality. Taupin believes Hulme transmitted these notions to the imagist poets,[52] and he is seconded here by Donald Davie: "I get the impression that Hulme's views about the nature of poetical language are the ideas most generally current, almost the standard ideas, among poets and their readers today, at least in the English-speaking world. . . . On the other hand, later writers have abandoned the Bergsonian element in Hulme's vocabularly, while often retaining, tacitly or unconsciously, his Bergsonian assumptions."[53] More circumspectly, Raymond points out a "kinship between speculative thought and literature."

> Correspondences can be established both in 1889 and in 1907 between the *Essai sur les données immédiates de la conscience and l'Évolution créatrice* on the one hand, and the condition of poetry, or a certain kind of poetry, in the respective periods. Bergsonism, which was auscultation of the self before it turned to the universe, seems to have developed along a curve parallel to that followed by the general development of literature in the same period.[54]

There will be occasion below to examine more carefully the "correspondences" Raymond mentions.

Not often, however, do critics analyze these influences or affinities in great detail, pointing, that is, to the ways in which the language has been physically marked in the attempt to capture an extraordinary state of consciousness or semiconsciousness. An exception is Davie's account of "subjective syntax." "Poetic syntax is subjective when its function is to please us by the fidelity with which it follows the "form of thought" in the poet's mind."[55] However, this critic cites passages from romantic poets who preserve, on the whole, the conventions of grammar. A shift in a train of thought may be marked by a suddenly expanded and elaborated subordinate clause. This technique, discussed above in the section devoted to elaboration, is but a preliminary step to more violent shifts and breaks in the language of poetry.

For a number of reasons, it seems likely that the fragment, in its various roles in poetry, serves best to translate many of the obscure processes of mental life with a minimum of distortion. Drawing from psychologist's theories of perception and cognition, from the observations of anthropologists on the languages of children and primitive cultures, and from literary critics with a penchant for introspection, one can show that there is ample justification for asyntactical, fragmented poetry, when the aim of such poetry is to express just that "unknown original" which Sapir thought inexpressible.

It has already been suggested that the noun, among all the parts of speech, retains a distinctly sensuous—and especially visual—quality. And the noun, of course, is commonly the kernel of a fragment in twentieth-century poetry. The great number of noun fragments in imagist poetry, as the very name of the school suggests, is surely an attempt to capitalize on this sensuous quality. "No other English poetry—no other poetry of the Western World—had hitherto been based so strictly on visual appeal." [56] Another observer, Babette Deutsch, says of the imagists, "They wanted words that would give unmistakably the sting of experience, endured and known. Hence the emphasis on the concrete detail—the object seen, heard, smelled, tasted and touched, on the metaphor that has the force of a physical sensation." [57] For "object" one may almost read "noun referring to what is seen. . . ."

Davie is probably right in tracing this predilection for concrete images to Fenellosa's seminal essay on Chinese and English poetry. He quotes Fenellosa's acute observation that the grammatical distinction between noun and verb is in any case a falsification of reality. "A true noun, an isolated thing, does not exist in nature. Things are only the terminal points, or rather the meeting points, of actions, cross-sections cut through actions, snapshots. Neither can a pure verb, an abstract motion, be possible in nature. The eye sees noun and verb as one: things in motion, motion in things, and so the Chinese conception tends to represent them." [58] Here an interesting question occurs to a reader of imagist poetry: If neither noun nor verb can exist independently "in nature," why rely principally on the noun to convey impressions? Why the image and not the action? Upon reflection, the reader discovers that while he can imagine—visualize—a bird or a deer, he cannot conceive of "flying" or "running" as disembodied activities. The word "bird" or "deer" strongly implies not only a static image, but a style of motion, just as a snapshot of these animals might suggest swiftness arrested. But to gather equally rich implications from verbs (unless, as Pound points out, they are formed from nouns: "to dog someone") [59] seems hardly possible. Interestingly enough, in many passages like the one quoted earlier from Pound's cantos, the imagist poets tried to fuse agent and action by turning verbs into participles subordinated to nouns. "Light shaking" is thus thought to convey a sustained visual experience better than "the light shakes" or "the light is shaking."

It is just here that the Bergsonian assumptions of modern poetry become apparent. For the French philosopher annihilated the distinctions of grammar and, to a degree, denied the efficacy of language as a valid expression of human consciousness. The "durée" allowed neither tense nor word order; it was "la succession sans la distinction." [60] Perception and sentiment melted into memory and memory in turn subtly pervaded them. This "multiplicité confuse" is the very essence of psychic life,[61] and to dissociate its elements, to substitute for "la pénétration des termes réels" "la juxtaposition de leurs symboles" is to destroy that essence. Thus, to seize "nos idées elles-mêmes à l'état naturel" one must shatter "les cadres du language." [62]

Nevertheless, Bergson gives poetry its due, and he traces the connections between feeling, image, and word. "Le poète est celui chez qui les sentiments se dévéloppent en images, et les images elles-mêmes en paroles, dociles au rythme, pour les traduire." [63] The most immediate, most concise "translation" of the image, again, is the noun with its attendant modifiers.

Catalogues furnish the best examples of fragments as replicas of immediate sense experience. Cleanth Brooks defines such poetry, after John Crowe Ransom's suggestion, as *physical poetry, a poetry of things without ideas*"; [64] about the early twentieth-century revolt from Victorianism he says,

> The poets attempt to do in one generation what it requires generations of poets to do. The result is a retreat toward the elementary undifferentiated "stuff" of poetry. Indeed, there is a great deal of primitivism to be found in the poetry of the revolt. With the rejection of formal verse systems there is a reversion to loose chant lines and repetition (Sandburg's "Chicago"); complex structure, logical or symbolical, gives way to the simple method of development by cumulative accretion—poems develop by the poets' piling up detail on detail (H. D.'s "Sea Gods"); raw "content" overrides and determines form. . . . [65]

The epithet "undifferentiated," in the light of Bergson's remarks, suggests that perhaps this "simple method" aims at reproducing something of the genuine quality of experience.

Of even more interest is the association of this technique with primitivism. There is good reason to believe that loose aggregates of concrete nouns which produce mental images—descriptive fragments—find a perfect parallel in the language of so-called primitive people, in the language of children, and possibly in certain "primitive" states of consciousness experienced by the highly civilized. Summarizing research by Gestalt psychologists, Franklin Fearing hypothesizes that pure *perception* constitutes the dawn of consciousness or cognition, and that "a primordial aspect of the structure of the percept is differentiation between figure and ground." [66] The concrete noun, as demonstrated, is unique in its ability to cast a shape onto the screen of consciousness, so that more than any other linguistic item it seems to me to reflect primordial experience, the fact that "we see things and not the holes between them." [67]

Finally, Fearing suggests that between pure perception and the interrelated abstractions of thought there is a kind of continuum through which moves, in stages, the developing mind of a child, or a developing culture, or any individual "perceptual process" regardless of age or culture. [68] The child and the savage establish a more immediate, sensuous contact with the world than does the man whose language continually meddles with his experience by synthesizing it into an abstract construct, and they may have trouble *differentiating* between their subjective reactions to what they perceive, and the perceived object itself.

Piaget has remarked this latter phenomenon among children; Redfield has substantiated the observation with regard to the mind of primitive man. [69] Benjamin Lee Whorf, whose theories were the bone of contention at the conference where Fearing presented his paper, has suggested that the "thought world" of the Hopi, shaped by certain features of his language, yields a conception of time rather different from that inherent in the "ways of speaking" common to most Indo-European languages. [70] In addition Whorf hints that metaphor may arise out of synesthesia, which he considers a nonlinguistic, primary mode of perception. Fearing, in turn—his position supported by the lifework of the psychologist Heinz Werner—links metaphor with the

131

primitive mind's confusion of objective stimulus and subjective experience, noting that in cultures dominated by Western science metaphor is "regarded with suspicion." [71] Indeed, the tendency toward "animism" (Piaget's term), toward viewing "objects as persons" (Redfield) has always infected poets' metaphors. In Sandburg's "Chicago," for example, the city is made into a "tool-maker" and "stacker of wheat." And for Whitman, grass is "the uncut hair of graves." "All the instruments agree" in Auden's elegy.

In an inquiry into the psychological nature of the whole literary process, from writer's brain to reader's, Wayne Shumaker concluded not only that poetic language is related to primitive, but that this relationship involves, specifically, a common preference for concrete terms and fragmentation, or "parataxis."

> It must by now be clear that the language of literature, in precisely those ways in which it differs from non-literary language, tends strikingly to resemble the languages spoken by many savages. It is concrete, specific, sensory, and it prefers the delineation of particular instances to the statement of abstract truths. It often registers percepts in clusters and does not, like the more consistently rational languages of philosophy and science, separate out for attention whatever strands of adjacent objects are conceptually related. On the contrary, it regards contiguity as proof of mutual involvement—"uncritically," it would appear to the logical thinker. The readiness to regard as connected whatever objects or ideas lie side by side is reflected also in a tendency toward paratactical syntax.[72]

To concreteness and parataxis, we might add the further parallel of "instinctive metaphor." Perhaps Shumaker means something of this sort when he speaks of "mutual involvement."

At any rate, the catalogue, or series of noun fragments, often does much more than describe, and much more, even, than simply represent as accurately as possible the electric immediacy of sensations. Whitman, Sandburg, Lawrence, Thomas, and the early Pound at times superimpose images very swiftly, so swiftly that the reader feels that he has, in fact, *perceived* one thing as another. The metaphor becomes a mode of perception, "adorning nature with a new thing." Thus Lawrence begins a poem entitled "Turkey-Cock,"

> You ruffled black blossom,
> You glossy dark wind.

And Pound's English hai-ku lines are already famous.

> The apparition of these faces in the crowd;
> Petals on a wet, black bough.

To be sure, none of these poets writes in this fashion all the time. And not all catalogues consist of a barrage of detail supposedly taken in on the spot by the poet's keen and roving eye, or of pairs of perceptions fused in the flash of instinctive metaphor. The "string of experience" is often absorbed and modified almost immediately by its context, so that a sentence may at any moment crystallize in the consciousness which the poem projects. Conversely, as in the structure labeled "disintegrating sentence," an ordered progression of thought may decay into a scattering of impressions, remembered or perhaps fanciful. But a typical fragment in a Whitman catalogue, both by position and punctuation, seems only one of a great rain of scarcely differentiated impingements on the senses, some new, some resurrected.

If the fragment is thus a matter of sensitive membranes, one may ask, why is it linked with the poetry born in the unconscious, in the "Unbewusste," in those "souterrains de la cité psychique"? Actually, the consciousness assimilates material from its depths as well as from its surface, where the immediate sense data are registered. Bergson recognized the fact when he spoke of the "profondeurs de la conscience," but restricted himself to an examination of sensation and sentiment *as they emerged* from whatever source. It also appears true that material from the unconscious, when it intrudes into awareness, is grasped in a manner not unlike the immediate cognition of the external world. A dream, for example, can sometimes bear a frightening resemblance to waking life. Here again the *visual quality* of dream, reverie, and poetic imagery associates these states with perception on the one hand and deeper levels of consciousness on the other.

Granted that sensorial acuity is indispensable to a poet, he still cannot be viewed as a camera of unusually fine adjustment. It has become apparent to students of linguistics, psychology, anthropology, and philosophy that a language is far from being an untroubled mirror of reality. A school of thinkers from Humboldt through Cassirer to Whorf has claimed that language *molds* perception. Cassirer quotes Humboldt as follows: "Dans la formation et dans l'usage de la langue passe nécessairement tout le caractère particulier de la perception des objets. Car le mot nait précisément de cette perception; il n'est pas une empreinte de l'objet en soi, mais de l'image que celui-ci engendre dans l'âme." [73] Cassirer adds later,

> Le langage n'entre pas dans un monde de perceptions objectives achevées, pour adjoindre seulement à des objets individuels donnés et clairement délimités les uns par rapport aux autres des "noms" qui seraient des signes purement extérieurs et arbitraires; mais il est lui-même un médiateur

134

dans la formation des objets; il est, en un sens, le
médiateur par excellence, l'instrument le plus important et le plus précieux pour la conquête et
pour la construction d'un vrai monde d'objets.[74]

Cassirer goes on to make the obvious connection between this conquering power of language and the tendency of children and primitive people to create in
words an imaginative universe—mytha inseparable
from the "real world."[75]

According to this view, just as the modes of perception govern in part the character of subjective experience, the individual mind, with language as its
mediator, infuses and distorts perception. The common
expression, "We see things differently," is an unusually
concise statement of the point, if we take the verb "see"
in all its senses. For still another reason, then, no such
thing as a "pure noun" or "pure verb" exists. One man's
happy noun is another's sad one. Because the link between perception and all other psychic activity is the
link of language, one hopes to find a grammatical model
of the continuum. The evidence suggests that the fragment, particularly the concrete noun, furnishes an element in such a model.

Models of the mind which involve spatial metaphors
have fallen into disrepute, but metaphors appear unavoidable in all but the most empirical sciences. To sum-
marize this discussion of the poetic process, we might
imagine a linear continuum from perception through
waking consciousness to the dream-world or frontier of
the unconscious. At either end of this continuum occur
largely visual images, or at least unverbalized sensations of one sort or another, while at the center there
exists a structured body of knowledge or ideas and a
corresponding body of grammatical utterances capable
of communicating this information—if, indeed, the
two are separate at all. Language permeates and unifies
all these aspects of experience. It may, however, alter

to express accurately the nature of a particular state of mind or a particular interaction among several such states.

It is an explicit principle in Freudian dream analysis that the unconscious manufactures images rather than words, and that the former ordinarily make up the "dream content" with which the consciousness is familiar. These images have the virtue of condensing an elaborate multiplicity of interrelated objects, feelings, and dialectic (the "dream-thoughts") into a unified impression—one assimilated almost literally at a glance.[76] In addition Freud believes that images displace words and provide thereby a rich system of interlocking, hidden meanings.

But the image-making power of the dream-work would help explain only the concreteness of language in poetry which draws on the unconscious. What of fragmentation? On the lack of grammatical coherence in dreams Freud comments directly; speaking of the train of dream-thoughts, he says,

> The individual parts of this complicated structure naturally stand in the most manifold logical relations to one another. They constitute foreground and background, digressions, illustrations, conditions, lines of argument and objections. When the whole mass of these dream-thoughts is subjected to the pressure of the dream-work, during which the fragments are turned about, broken up and compacted, somewhat like drifting ice, the question arises, what becomes of the logical ties which had hitherto provided the framework of the structure? What representation do "if," "because," "as though," "although," "either . . . or" and all the other conjunctions, without which we cannot understand a phrase or a sentence, receive in our dreams?

To begin with, we must answer that the dream

has at its disposal no means of representing these logical relations between the dream-thoughts. In most cases it disregards all these conjunctions, and undertakes the elaboration only of the material content of the dream thoughts. It is left to the interpretation of the dream to restore the coherence which the dream-work has destroyed.[77]

It might be argued that restoring the coherence of the dream-thoughts in turn destroys the poetic quality of the dream. At any rate, many of the recent poets in this study abandon not only conjunctions but even verbs, so that what remains is not discourse but a patterning of images. Even when syntactic forms persist, as Davie points out, they may "carry no weight" of poetic meaning.[78] But at other times, as in the fused structures in Eliot, a fragment may operate in two contexts, so that syntax is made to bear a unique poetic meaning.

Concrete nouns, often fragmentary, therefore function as a partial transcript of the material of the subconscious; just as one kind of fragment strives to represent the immediacy of imaginative perception, other kinds attempt to imitate the unmediated products of subconscious mental activity. These products also include remembered utterances somehow altered and, on the borderline of consciousness, that nascent thought that marks the utmost limit of the dramatic monologue.

In making use of fragments, a poet accomplishes the same kind of condensation and displacement that Freud observed in dream-work. Unlike a mere perception, the image from the unconscious brings with it a host of associations which may interact with those inherent in other images, and in such a way that no syntactical relation could truly express the interaction in all its subtlety. Fidelity to the character of dream consciousness, or of madness, precludes a regular sentence pattern in some poems. D. H. Lawrence says of a poem of

137

his designed to capture the quality of Ophelia's insanity, "Don't you see the poor thing is cracked, and she used all those verses—apples and chickens and rat —according to true instinctive or *dream* symbolism. This poem—I am very proud of it—has got the quality of a troublesome dream that seems incoherent but is selected by another sort of consciousness. The latter part is the waking up part—yet never really awake, because she is mad." [79] Lawrence's epistolary prose, like Pound's, contains interruptions and fragments just as his poetry does.

One faces here in somewhat different terms the problem of the inexpressible. As Susanne Langer observes, "Language in its ordinary use is peculiarly inadequate for the articulation of subjective facts, such as the dynamic form of an emotion." [80] Hence the poet's attempts to "dislocate language . . . into his meaning," [81] as Eliot puts it, or "to find, to invent, the special language which will alone be capable of expressing his personality and feelings," in the words of Edmund Wilson.[82] To outline the potential resources of such a language lies beyond the bounds of this study, but surely fused structures, disintegrating sentences, and the fragments interwoven among such structures are attempts to find linguistic equivalents for experiences which cannot be represented by the language as it is ordinarily used. The disintegrating sentence may reflect the unpredictable shift from formulated thought to reverie or to simple awareness of sensation; the fused structure betrays a like shift from one vision to another, as when Eliot's "typist home at teatime" vanishes from one sentence to materialize in the next—reminding one, perhaps, of those dreams in which one moves through many different contexts without being aware of the transitions. And fragments merely juxtaposed suggest relations ineffable, though sensed, and preserve an irreducible richness, variety, and immediacy in their mutual interaction.

138

On a more obvious level, the noun fragment compares with the dream image because it signifies but does not assert. Even the "descriptive" fragment which appears to convey only a sense impression is actually laden with significance for the perceiving mind. The mind, again, is no camera. What Pongs says of symbols could be extended to any word which flowers into image.

> Im Sinnbild *fallen* Sinn und Bild zusammen. Zugleich aber weist der im Bild gemeinte Sinn weit über das Bild hinaus.[83]

> . . . wie man logisch sagt: *es ist* und *es bedeutet!* Zugleich aber geht diese Repräsentation über jedes logische Begreifen hinaus. Sie vergegenwärtigt etwas, was sich logisch nicht fassbar machen lasst, und sie vergegenwärtigt es in lebendig augenblicklicher Offenbarung.[84]

Though English does not hint at the identity as German does, for a poet whatever is, means. No perception is for him pure, and his individual mind—which is not simply coextensive with his language but includes it—inheres actively in the entire continuum of the psychic process. If language distorts perception, making of it metaphorical vision, and passion shapes language—as in the dramatic monologue—then passion itself, if it is to be represented, must appear as images dense with whole arguments and multiple associations; for intense feelings are always a gathering, a concentration of forces. The image, then, as the "smallest unit of perception," is also the smallest unit of meaning in any representation of the complexity of psychic life, particularly of emotion.

Working directly and deliberately with these units of perception, to transform them into a record of experience at the deepest levels of consciousness, poets began to rely as much upon invisible associations as upon syntactic links. Thus, juxtaposition of images, usually fragments, has perhaps more than any other single stylistic trait earned for modern poetry its reputation for obscurity. In part this obscurity arises because a group of images bound by invisible associations may evoke a certain emotion whose very nature cannot be stated and whose effect depends on the devaluation of individual images as units of distinct meaning. To the poet, an image in the company of certain other images may concentrate a feeling which has little to do with the meaning of the words outside this context. Then dictionaries are of no help.

This poetry seems to attempt to render the immediate products of the mind, whether in the form of speech or in the form of a sequence of images. The activity of the mind itself, from perception through everyday conceptualization to dream-making in the abyss of the unconscious, is an organic and continuous process. The perceived image is distilled into language, or, passing into the maelstrom of the unconscious, is impregnated there with emotion as part of a "felt form," a construct of feeling with its own principle of organization. These roles of the image are inseparable in poetry, and only by the arrangement of verbal symbols can the artist indicate which segment of the psychic continuum he is representing. That many modern poets employ colloquial word order and concrete noun fragments suggests that they are at various times trying to imitate the assimilation of immediate sense data, the spontaneous formation of thoughts to be uttered, and the coalescing of mental images, that is, the first product of emotional forces underlying consciousness. Or poets may attempt to represent a medley of these psychic activities. Seldom, in fact, is one conscious of the predominance of any one of them or even of distinctions between them. A complex and sustained emotion almost always involves the whole range of psychic activity.

It is necessary to stress that evidence drawn from Bergson, Freud, and other introspectionists from diverse disciplines, like Heinz Werner, Cassirer, Hermann Pongs, Whorf, and Jung, supports the view that this poetry strives to represent or imitate mental life. Now, our civilized and scientific intellects carefully categorize the self and the world, relating the two only by grammatical statements which often turn out to be, *au fond*, rough translations of formulae. Language thus becomes a symbolic model of physical relationships. Einstein gives to language this role.[85] The poet, however, may seek to represent raw perceptions unworked by the logical faculties. Or he may superimpose fragments in a sudden and violent metaphor which confuses fact and feeling, self and world, after the fashion of children and savages. Yet even the adult "civilized" consciousness is fed by perceptions, and may work in a primitive fashion before being purged by the active intellect, responsive to the exigencies of a scientific culture. Finally, the poet may find inspiration in dreams, or in dreamlike states, which appear to be beyond the control of logic; their linguistic counterpart is a mixture of everyday discourse (remembered conversations) quite possibly out of context, and disconnected noun phrases (images of the dream-work) in a combination whose significance is hidden and therefore asyntactic. To impose rigid syntax on this apparent hodgepodge would actually falsify experience, as the mind often undergoes it.

In one sense, poets like Browning and Whitman and their stylistic inheritors attempt an empirical accuracy beyond the grasp of science. They shape language to reflect and even reproduce all kinds of experience. They recreate with words that puzzling movie inside our heads, whose scenes dissolve, break off, and becomes distorted according to certain laws of interplay between latent awareness and the unconscious. Certainly, this preoccupation with representing the very stuff of human existence is a "scientific" aim of sorts, though its product, the poem, manages a fusion of objective and subjective that science cannot duplicate.

Designed as they are to achieve utmost fidelity to the form of psychic processes, these changes in the language of poetry betray a concern for realism. In this light, modern poetry is a part of the dominant current in twentieth-century literature and akin to novel, play, or film as well as to experimental music and painting. The film, a visual medium not strictly bound to any temporal sequence of images, may have particularly close parallels with modern poetry. (A recent paper by Neal Oxenhandler, for example, suggests that the movie *Jules and Jim* is constructed according to the *ars poetica* of Guillaume Apollinaire.[86]) In fact, when novelists and playwrights discovered that "reality" was no more than an individual's psychic life, of which reason was but a part (*Ulysses, Strange Interlude*), poets had already developed formal techniques to render the quality of subjective experience. In this way the most potent ideas of the modern era—the romantic fascination for the irrational, the scientific respect for precise sense data accurately recorded, and the belief that reality in space and time is entirely relative to individual viewpoint—converge in a great deal of modern poetry.[87]

This convergence is manifest in the implicit belief among so many poets that abstractions sin against the higher truth of the sensitive membrane, that a stark image radiates emotional forces not to be paraphrased, that, on the whole, the mind is an autonomous process far exceeding, in diversity and subtlety, the range of expression in ordinary speech.

6

Syntax in the Poem

BY INTRODUCING regular and fragmentary structures, modern poets achieve a special kind of realism, but it would be wrong to suggest that every such structure seeks this effect. One can seldom determine to what degree individual poets deliberately strive to model their verse after a philosophical notion of reality. If he could, writing literary history would be an easier task. What has been offered here, a count of common types of sentence variation in certain major poets, serves as evidence not of a conscious, common purpose in poetry but of one of those glacial shifts in style upon whose causes and course one can but speculate. Interesting as such speculation is, it does not aid a reader to deal with most particular poems.

Nevertheless, to reiterate an assumption obviously necessary to this study, the patterning of words determines style as does their choice and their "linked sweetness" of sound. And a poet's style is in turn responsible for effects upon the reader; it tickles, soothes, shocks, or charms him or, sometimes, merely puzzles him. The study of syntax in individual poems, then, may facilitate an understanding of the ways in which they move readers. How does the construction—or destruction—of sentences contribute to a poem's effect, along with its diction, meter, and stanzaic pattern?

To illustrate the question, one may compare two rather undistinguished poems on the same subject.

What great yoked brutes with briskets low,
With wrinkled necks like buffalo,
With round, brown, liquid, pleading eyes,
That turn'd so slow and sad to you.
That shone like love's eyes soft with tears
That seem'd to plead, and make replies,
The while they bow'd their necks and drew
The creaking load; and looked at you.
Their sable briskets swept the ground,
Their cloven feet kept solemn sound.

Two sullen bullocks led the line,
Their great eyes shining bright like wine;
Two sullen captive kings were they,
That had in time held herds at bay,
And even now they crush'd the sod
With stolid sense of majesty,
And stately stepp'd and stately trod,
As if 'twere something still to be
Kings even in captivity.[1]

—Joaquin Miller

A YOKE OF STEERS

A heave of mighty shoulders to the yoke,
Square, patient heads, and flaring sweep of horn;
The darkness swirling down beneath their feet
Where sleeping valleys stir, and feel the dawn;
Uncouth and primal, on and up they sway,
Taking the summit in a drench of day.
The night-winds volley upward bitter-sweet,
And the dew shatters to a rainbow spray
Under the slow-moving, cloven feet.
There is a power here that grips the mind;
A force repressed and inarticulate,
Slow as the swing of centuries, as blind

here contributes in some way to the effect for which the poet strives.

The second poem begins with fragments much different from those in the first. There are four such fragments, all clearly independent of one another, all rather short. Unlike Miller's carefully connected phrases and clauses, these four noun phrases are merely juxtaposed; their mutual relations are so implicitly clear that the poet need not signal them grammatically. Only the last noun, "darkness," with its extensive modification, betrays this consistent economy. The clauses which shift the reader's attention to awakening valleys indeed seem to dilute the immediacy and precision of the synoptic sketch of a team of oxen. However, this slight straying and expansion may have a function in the poem, a point to which I shall return in a moment.

After thus merely posing certain details, the poet makes three direct statements, the first of which contains a mild dislocation ("on and up they sway"), and the remaining two of which, quite regular, may strike the reader as digressive or as gratuitous scenery at best. The assertions, however, are too independent and too vigorous to function well as sheer "description"; as pure decor the dew and night winds might have been slipped in by adding a phrase to the first sentence. Instead, the poet appears to be gathering his first, scattered impressions of the ox team toiling up a mountain in order to organize them into a narrative sequence. In rapid succession the oxen take the sun-drenched summit, the night winds "volley," and the dew "shatters to a rainbow spray" in the morning light. The statements have superficial semantic links with one preceding fragment: "darkness" = "nightwinds," "dawn" = "day" = "rainbow," "down beneath their feet" = "on and up." But more important, the verbs in these statements transform what first seems a collection of vagabond impressions into a complex of very nearly simultaneous, dynamic, and related activities. The use of a direct, vigorous but uncomplicated sentence form here reinforces the connotation of the verbs themselves; for "volley" and "shatter" are violent, instantaneous actions. The poet exploits these connotations further, I think, in the next sentence.

If in the last three sentences of the first stanza Heyward attains something like Fenellosa's ideal of "motion in things, things in motion," communicating both the suddenness and the force with which the oxen "top out" in a crash of sunlight, wind and dewspray; he changes his style abruptly in the next stanza—coextensive with the next sentence. The poem's only elaborate structure, this sentence begins with a suggestion of rhetorical flourish and moves in a measured cadence. Its length, the four or five pauses in its development, the dislocated adjectives in line eleven—all these accord well with its meaning. The locution "there is," suggesting the timeless and immutable, is a structural complement of the phrase "slow as the swing of centuries" and a perfect contrast to the suddenness of "shatters."

Yet this magisterial and philosophical statement, and the conclusion which follows from it in the next sentence, grow naturally enough out of sketchy images and their coalescence into a single, brief but sustained vision of the oxen as they conquer a ridge. From the first line, in fact, Heyward has stressed indirectly the relentless strength of the beasts, in preparation for his eventual conclusion that in them dwells also a spiritual power of immense scope and grandeur. The oxen first appear to the reader as a "heave of mighty shoulders" and a "flaring sweep of horn." The last fragment, with its clausal extension introducing the "sleeping valleys" which "stir and feel the dawn," amplifies this stress—however weakly—in so far as the stirring life and dawn imply an awakening in all nature of that same power that drives the mighty shoulders beneath the yoke. In

148

the next three sentences this power becomes active, explicit: the team sways up to "take" or conquer the summit; the winds volley bittersweet—as if in protest mingled with praise—and dew shatters under hooves. This crescendo of relentless force brings the poem near to its climax: the brawn of oxen is to be raised by a "power"—to the level of an eternal, impersonal, and unconquerable life-force. The solemnity of this operation, the hint of religiosity, require for expression a certain formality and elaborateness of statement. The middle stanza marks, then, a shift from language designed to communicate a striking experience to the language of reflection upon such experience. I call this shift "natural" because pantheistic philosophies normally proceed first from flower to dogma, and only afterwards the other way about.

The next-to-last sentence follows logically from the middle stanza, being a specific application of the general principle just derived. Also this sentence provides a variation on the main theme, for the phrase "unhurried by the goads of lesser wills" tells us that the awesome power of the oxen is not only timeless and inexorable but also superhuman. At the same time, by returning the reader's attention to the team and its burdens, Heyward diminishes slightly their cosmic significance and thereby manages a gradual relaxation of the intensity of the preceding two stanzas. The poem really ends here, with a sentence neither unbuttoned nor beribboned, but plain, calm and firm. The last line is merely unfortunate. It makes of a power supposedly as impressive as time or fate something local and vegetable.

In spite of its defects, Heyward's poem accommodates syntax to artistic purpose while Miller mismatches the two. The progression from fragments through direct and streamlined sentences to elaborate statement, and back to a regular sentence neither passionate nor pompous in form, corresponds to the development of thought out of experience and the subsequent return of that thought upon the experience. Miller, on the other hand, elaborates uncritically, introducing essentially peripheral or even irrelevant details. He makes forceful and independent what ought to be unobtrusive and supplementary. Consequently, except in the last lines, his poem has no aesthetically meaningful syntactic structure. But syntax, like rhyme, cannot be neutral. It must impose a pattern that either detracts from or enhances poetic merit. Miller's poem illustrates clearly enough the disaster of ill-fitting syntax.

One finds this pattern in a good many lyrics: a fragment or two introduces the reader to those perceptions, usually visual images, out of which develop more highly organized intellectual processes—judgments, comparisons, and the formulation of philosophical principles. The poet attempts to convince his readers of the truth of his statements by revealing how solidly rooted in experience, in the heard and seen, such statements are. An elementary example occurs in Hardy's poem "In Time of 'The Breaking of Nations.'"

> Only a man harrowing clods
>   In a slow silent walk
> With an old horse that stumbles and nods
>   Half asleep as they stalk.
>
> Only a thin smoke without flame
>   From the heaps of couch-grass;
> Yet this will go onward the same
>   Though Dynasties pass.
> Yonder a maid and her wight
>   Come whispering by:
> War's annals will cloud into night
>   Ere their story die.[3]

From one glimpse of the rustic round, Hardy can derive a measure of hope for the future of mankind.

Obviously, he singles out of a whole panorama only the most pregnant details. The plowman and the incessant, inexorable, natural process of oxidation are subtly equated; so that the "this" of the middle stanza refers indiscriminately to either. The eternal changelessness of plowing and of burning is emphasized by the absence of verbs, which would limit and arrange these actions in time; and the connotations of "slow," "silent," and "old" reinforce this impression. The last stanza proceeds to a further contrast between nature and the spurious artifices of civilization; but since this contrast occurs entirely on the human plane, complete sentences are employed—as if to launch, in fact, a narrative account, a deathless "story." The point Hardy is making resembles that Heyward arrives at in the poem previously quoted: there are unconquerable life-forces that move around and through puny individual man. Both poets employ like syntactic patterns to dramatize the thought forcefully.

An example of the use of this same pattern for a less easily definable purpose occurs in a poem of Denise Levertov's.

THE FIVE DAY RAIN

The washing hanging from the lemon tree
in the rain
and the grass long and coarse.

Sequence broken, tension
of bitter-orange sunlight
frayed off.

So light a rain
fine shreds
pending above the rigid leaves.

Wear scarlet! Tear the green lemons
off the tree! I don't want

> to forget who I am, what has burned in me,
> and hang limp and clean, an empty dress—[4]

Six fragments mostly descriptive are followed by three regular sentences. What are their connections? This time one cannot claim that the sentences constitute a ready inference from the experience represented by the fragments. It is not clear how a vision of a washing hung in the rain could provoke the fervent desire to preserve one's identity, or what coarse grass has to do with an insistence on wearing red.

However, the poem becomes intelligible—or feelable—if we regard the fragments as an attempt to communicate a perception, not a "pure" perception but one of those along with which we usually experience an emotion. Now ordinarily after a hot spell people are relieved to have the "tension of bitter-orange sunlight frayed off." If the banality of the expression be overlooked, one can read not only relief but a kind of mindless quiescence into a phrase applied to the coming of rain: it "settles the dust," the dust of human strife. A light rain without a wind or thunder makes the landscape still and gray; it washes away the traces of toil, brings peace, perhaps lethargy, but usually a vague sense of both relaxation and renewal.

The last stanza revolts against just these feelings. The "I" of the poem demands scarlet, not greenery, calls even for the destruction of the unripe lemons. The speaker apparently feels threatened by the monotonous rain or, rather, the state of mind rain induces; apparently, in the fashion described by some as "primitive," she can find her own feelings expressed by a limp, hanging dress. This immediate sensation—one has heard others speak of a "washed-out" feeling—she rejects, clamoring instead for self-conscious memories, for the recollection of passion—fire instead of water, "what has burned in me."

In the absence of clear syntactic signals, however,

the reader must attempt to comprehend this poem by simply allowing the isolated words in it to work upon his emotions. If, like the "I" of the poem, he can respond emotionally to rain and an empty dress, and if he associates antonymous emotions with scarlet gowns and fire, he can then understand the nature of the violent rejection and choice expressed in the last lines. The meaning one discovers here does not emerge as a philosophical comment directly applicable to the experience dealt with in the poem, as in Hardy, where of course meaning emerges like a whale surfacing. The sharp commands in Levertov's poem are a reaction to emotions which have merely been assumed to inhere in certain experiences. The language of the commands relates to the words rendering the sheer experience only by "associations" left unstated. It is perfectly possible that many minds do not form these associations. Readers possessed of such minds may justifiably accuse the poet of obscurity.

Thus, despite its simplicity of structure, the fragment may produce subtle effects. But a number of poets, Whitman, Lawrence, and Pound among them, employ the device primarily to describe with telegraphic economy. As mere description, the fragment tends to become wearisome and flat. Witness Pound's fragments linked by simple repetition:

Glass-glint of wave in the tide-rips against sunlight
Pallor of Hesperus,
Grey peak of the wave,
    Wave, colour of grape's pulp,

Olive grey in the near,
    far, smoke grey of the rock-slide. . . .[5]

Such chains of visual images are actually not much different in pattern from some exhaustive descriptions in

older poetry. In the February 1850 issue of *Blackwood's,*
for example, a poet wrote,

> A GLORIOUS amphitheatre, whose girth
> Exceeds three-fold the horizons of the north
> Mixing our pleasure in a goblet wide,
> With hard, firm rim through clear air described;
> Illumined mountains, on whose heavenly slopes,
> Quick busy shades rehearse, while Phoebus drops,
> Dramatic parts in scenic mysteries. . . .[6]

And so on for another twenty-four lines. The similarity
in shape of amphitheatre, goblet, and encircling mountain range provides the excuse for juxtaposing these
images, just as the translucence of glass, grapes, and
sea justifies Pound's sequence. The digressive clauses
introducing "Phoebus" and "busy shades" indeed en-
cumber the simple metaphor, and Pound saw fit to
eliminate such frills once thought pretty; but the fundamental principle of simply adding noun to noun, like
dabs of paint to canvas, is the same in both poets.

Levertov's technique, on the other hand, is to suddenly fuse what seem to be descriptive fragments into
the emotional atmosphere of a poem, as it is established
throughout by the connotation of words and the tone of
their utterance. Often the pattern of her poem can be
seen, on a lesser scale, in a few lines of a longer work.
Eliot prefaces one of his pious assertions, for example,
with the swift notation of a physiological reaction which
in part generated the pronouncement.

> My friend, blood shaking my heart
> The awful daring of a moment's surrender
> Which an age of prudence can never retract
> By this, and this only, we have existed. . . .[7]

The fragment or nominative absolute "blood shaking
my heart" furnishes evidence of the raw emotional state

out of which religious conviction, rationally stated, grows. In an earlier passage, the poet condenses his bitter contempt for the great unwashed into a fragmentary "quotation."

> . . . yet there the nightingale
> Filled all the desert with inviolable voice
> And still she cried, and still the world pursues,
> 'Jug Jug' to dirty ears.[8]

In the midst of merely describing a picture portraying the Philomela story, without any preparation, Eliot mocks the viewpoint of those coarse and insensitive people who fail to find the poignant beauty of legend in a bird's call. The "Jug Jug" is clearly the eruption of a prejudice, cryptically phrased, without syntactical or "logical" relevance to the preceding sentence. Since this prejudice crops up again in the poem, however, the reader suspects that a coherent set of values, or attitudes, underlies such apparently disorganized material. He is forced, however, to seek order in linguistic structures larger than a sentence—as large, even, as an entire poem.

One can find numerous illustrations of such sophisticated harmony between syntax and the other elements of a poem. Lest it appear that the elaborate sentence has no use at all in modern poetry, consider the clever effects Auden produces in "Musée des Beaux Arts" by means of this device.

> About suffering they were never wrong,
> The Old Masters; how well they understood
> Its human position; how it takes place
> While someone else is eating or opening a window
>   or just walking dully along;
> How, when the aged are reverently, passionately
>   waiting
> For the miraculous birth, there always must be

Children who did not specially want it to happen,
    skating
On a pond at the edge of the wood.
They never forgot
That even the dreadful martyrdom must run its
    course
Anyhow in a corner, some untidy spot
Where the dogs go on with their doggy life and
    the torturer's horse
Scratches its innocent behind on a tree.
In Brueghel's *Icarus*, for instance: how everything
    turns away
Quite leisurely from the disaster; the ploughman
    may
Have heard the splash, the forsaken cry,
But for him it was not an important failure; the
    sun shone
As it had to on the white legs disappearing into
    the green
Water; and the expensive delicate ship that must
    have seen
Something amazing, a boy falling out of the sky,
Had somewhere to get to and sailed calmly on.[9]

The dislocation with which Auden begins this poem
has an oddly colloquial flavor; it is as if another party
had just mentioned "suffering," and the poet in his re-
joinder had picked up the key word, maintaining emphasis on it by putting it first in the sentence despite a
resulting inversion of normal word order. The two elaborations—one of them double—which follow, extending over eleven lines, complete the stanza. Does not
this sudden elaboration by clauses depart from the colloquial tone first struck? To a degree it does; but the
poet has by the opening dislocation established that
the speaker in the poem chats with some elegance. Further, the two noun clauses in the second sentence
("how it takes place . . ." and "how . . . there always

must be . . .") are in loose apposition to "human position." They thus have a certain rambling independence; they are clearly additive and explanatory, tending to garrulity rather than complexity. The commonplace adverbs "just," "specially," "anyhow" also minimize any literary pretensions the constructions might entail.

These elaborate structures, in fact, reinforce a major theme of the poem—an ironic disparity between the importance of events and the triviality of their setting. The poet ostensibly sets out to discuss suffering from the point of view of one who knows its true significance, knows the birth is "miraculous," the martyrdom "dreadful." But clauses introduce the mundane in shocking detail. Extensive and vivid, as opposed to the terse, neutral notation of "[suffering] takes place" and "martyrdom must run its course," they dramatize the ironic contrast which the poet is even here pointing out. The indifferent children skate, the horse scratches its behind—these activities, structurally "subordinate" to statements about suffering, subvert our attention to those statements; similarly, in Brueghel's painting the eye is led away from this "principal" subject to its surroundings, which are elaborated in detail and given a prominent position. The imbalance is reinforced by a contrast between the concrete diction reserved for the insignificant and the shapeless jargon used for the portentous; between children "skating on a pond at the edge of the wood" and "miraculous birth."

The second stanza performs a final neat maneuvre. The fragments with which the stanza opens maintain the colloquial note, for the "how" clause appears to be an afterthought which the speaker meant to append in parallel fashion to the two noun clauses in his first rambling statement. A whole sentence of different construction, of course, has been uttered in the meantime. But now the specific instance which has occurred to him is so perfect an illustration of the point that he is moved to adopt the dispassionate style of a passerby, as if to parody the viewpoint of the plowman. In matter-of-fact language he relates the three incidents on which the painter has concentrated: the plowman heard a cry, the sun shone, the ship sailed calmly on. Icarus is reduced to a pair of legs twinkling into the sea within the confines of a prepositional phrase, or to "something" amazing which idle sailors happen to glimpse. This final irony depends in part on Auden's having chosen peripheral agents and actions as the main subjects and verbs of these three regular and almost reportorial sentences. Indiscriminate journalism is substituted for tragic poetry.

Not only do modern poets exercise liberty in their ordering and disordering of sentence elements, they often disregard the usual grammatical meaning of individual words. They do not feel bound to make syntax consonant with morphology; they use adjectives, prepositions or adverbs as subjects of sentences; and nouns as adverbs or adjectives. The language permits a degree of such flexibility, but many poets otherwise dissimilar go far beyond precedent in their disrespect for grammatical categories. The tendency is widespread:

> Christ follows Dionysus,
> Phallic and ambrosial
> Made way for macerations; [10]

> A cool of books
> will sometimes lead the mind to libraries
> of a hot afternoon. . . .[11]

> On neither side let foot slip over
> Invading always, exploring Never,
> For this is hate and this is fear.[12]

> angelheaded hipsters burning for the ancient heavenly connection to the starry dynamo in the machinery of night,

158

> who poverty and tatters and hollow-eyed and high
>> sat up smoking in the supernatural dark-
>> ness . . .
> who were expelled from the academies for crazy
>> & publishing obscene odes on the win-
>> dows of the skull . . .[13]

In Pound's lines, the adjectives "phallic" and "ambro-sial" are used as nouns, from which, to be sure, they were originally derived. Williams likewise nominalizes "cool," while Auden makes objects of verbs of two adverbs. Ginsberg makes "poverty and tatters" into adjectives, "crazy" into a noun. Just what nuance the poet gains by this kind of juggling is difficult to determine. Adding a "the" before Pound's adjectives would regularize his sentence; a suffix would render Williams' statement unobtrusive. But the sense of Auden's noun-adverbs could hardly be reproduced in another form. "Always" and "never" are absolute conditions for which we have no ready synonyms. As in Cummings' "pretty How town," these words assume in their unfamiliar roles a scarcely paraphrasable new meaning.

Stevens attempts even more radical experiments along these lines. The point of a little poem "Table Talk" depends directly on the violence done to a verb in the first stanza:

> Granted, we die for good.
> Life, then, is largely a thing
> Of happens to like, not should.[14]

By introducing a headless sentence as if it were a thing, the poet communicates a number of nuances at a stroke. "Happens to like," as a subjectless and objectless verb, appears to have universal and indiscriminate application; it is not individual, not directed. At the same time —no small feat—it expresses a preference active and subjective. The extreme economy by which a whole doctrine of relativistic epicureanism is compressed into this idiomatic verb, and an opposing system of ethical imperatives into a mere piece of a verb ("should") is in itself a powerful irony. The profoundest of philosophical disputes is resolved in an epigram delivered between bites of roast beef.

In *The Man With the Blue Guitar* Stevens again exploits the subtleties of this unorthdox shift.

> Is it ideas that I believe?
> Good air, my only friend, believe,
>
> Believe would be a brother full
> Of love, believe would be a friend,
>
> Friendlier than my only friend,
> Good air.[15]

Here another disembodied verb, "believe," has been used in three different ways in the space of four lines. Once the verb is used as part of a predicate, with a subject in the first person singular; twice it appears itself as a subject; what grammatical function it fulfills in line two one is rather at a loss to say, but surely there the word behaves differently than it does in its other two roles. At any rate, the effect of these four lines is to transmute a verb into something simultaneously verb and subject, no less than either but different from both. To accomplish this verbal prestidigitation, the poet suspends the word, in line two, as if it were a fragment without perceptible grammatical ties to a sentence. Then he slyly repeats the word, this time giving it an unambiguous but wholly unexpected function in a new sentence. In retrospect, the "believe" of line two may appear to act as an appositive equivalent to the "believe" which begins the next stanza. But, fortunately, the explication of the trick comes too late to spoil its magic.

What special significance does "believe" have as a friendly brother that can never be? If one substitutes "belief" or "to believe," the normal nominative forms of the concept, a nuance is lost. "Belief" implies a thorough commitment to a specific code or system; the infinitive is the most general and impersonal of notions. The finite verb form, on the other hand, maintains something of the fervor of personal involvement without allowing this impulse to settle on any object. The hint of an absent first-person subject suggests a vague yearning, the total absence of an object implies its frustration. However desirable the state of believing may be, the poet cannot fasten on any belief. By invoking this daring truncation of a statement as an active agent in his life, to which he can respond with feelings of brotherhood and friendship, Stevens communicates the sense of a rare psychological state: the wistfully vicarious experiencing of intensely personal emotions which stem from attitudes the poet can only imagine, attitudes which, since he cannot adopt them, must remain wholly undefined as to circumstance and detail. The powerfully emotive but deliberately vague language, ("love," "brother," "friend," "good") and the conditional form with the condition significantly omitted—no "if" clause follows the "would"—enhance the tone of indefinable longing, the sense of an awareness of experiences doomed to remain hypothetical.

It is Stevens, perhaps, who most skillfully combines sentences in a regular pattern with generous quantities of fragments. Yet seldom does he attempt to accomplish this fusion by representing directly the flux of consciousness. There are traces of colloquialism in his work, distantly related perhaps to techniques of the dramatic monologue: "till" instead of "until," "that's" for "that is" and occasional interjections; but fused and disintegrating structures are not common, and one finds few of the dashes, dots, line breaks, and so on that other poets use to convey the abrupt transitions of undisciplined consciousness. To label his fragments purely "descriptive" would also constitute an injustice. He is not guilty of what Yvor Winters calls the "imitative fallacy," for often his poetry is *about* the struggle to avoid that same fallacy, to present not "things as they are" but things transformed by the poetic sensibility.

In a few of Stevens' poems, these very fundamental issues concerning language and its relation to perception, and thus to the world as we know it, have been directly confronted. One is thus given the unique opportunity to judge theory and practice in a single performance. For instance, evidence was cited earlier for the noun fragment's effectiveness in conveying, almost simultaneously, a sense impression and a complex modification of that impression by the mind and emotions. The poem "What We See Is What We Think" corroborates that evidence rather explicitly.

> At twelve, the disintegration of afternoon
> Began, the return to phantomerei, if not
> To phantoms. Till then, it had been the other way.
>
> One imagined the violet trees but the trees stood
>   green,
> At twelve, as green as ever they would be.
> The sky was blue beyond the vaultiest phrase.
>
> Twelve meant as much as: the end of normal time,
> Straight up, an elan without harrowing,
> The imprescriptible zenith, free of harangue,
>
> Twelve and the first gray second after, a kind
> Of violet gray, a green violet, a thread
> To weave a shadow's leg or sleeve, a scrawl
>
> On the pedestal, an ambitious page dog-eared
> At the upper right, a pyramid with one side
> Like a spectral cut in its perception, a tilt

162

And its tawny caricature and tawny life,
Another thought, the paramount ado . . .
Since what we think is never what we see.[16]

Without explicating in detail, one may still understand generally the manner in which the diction and
syntactic structure of this poem help to substantiate the
claims it makes concerning the nature of the mind's
experience. As the title and last line suggest, the poet
here holds that perception automatically involves distortion—the mind deals not with replicas but with its
own creations. Only at high noon, when no shadows
interfere, can the eye give an accurate account of the
world; one second after the disintegration again becomes manifest. Fittingly enough the first two stanzas,
beginning presumably precisely "at twelve," develop in
perfectly regular, straightforward sentences. They are
statements of utter lucidity, without shadow. No others
are possible: one may try to imagine violet trees, but
at noon the trees stand green, and the sky is an incon-
trovertible and indescribable blue. For an instant
there is no place for figurative language in experience;
at the "imprescriptible zenith" things are "free of
harangue."
     Then, however, the transparent language of the poem
begins to alter. The third stanza lanuches a list of what
one might call almost-fragments. These structures form
a most interesting pattern. The key nouns in stanza
three: "end," "elan," "zenith," fit reasonably well into
the structure of the preceding sentence, as comple-
ments of the verb "meant." In the next two stanzas,
however, we encounter additional noun phrases whose
function is not so clear. Surely one would not read
"Twelve meant as much as twelve," for example. These
additional elements, then, may be fragments. There is
another change. The language of stanza three remains
abstract: "end," "time," "elan," "zenith," "straight up"
refer to states and conditions, not things. But in the

163

next stanza, corresponding to the waning of the after-noon, the language gains color, density, shape. Out of grayness and greenness confused—incipient shadow—a thread of outline is spun; the thread sketches a leg or sleeve as a pointer throws a scrawl on the sundial; then, in a rush, the mind moves out of its one instant of mirror blankness—the image of the sundial resolves into others of man's efforts in time, his books and monu-ments. But even as these images are born, rooted so intimately in a keen perception (the three-corneredness of pointer, crimped page, pyramid face, unites them), imagination has transmuted them into metaphor. And as the poem draws to its end, the metaphor grows less sensual, more intellectual: "another thought," "the para-mount ado" replace the sundial, page, and pyramid, already reduced to a "tilt and its tawny life."

Logical syntax does not, however, return immediately with abstract diction. As metaphor springs mysteriously full-blown from visual impression, so thought appears, final distillate, as an inexplicable product of experience in the dimension of time. The eye organizes, too sum-marily for thought to follow; but thought in turn seems to shape itself, and then the eye must acquiesce. The eye is also fanciful, for shadows alter "things" and shadows arc the eye's creation. Night indeed makes monsters of tree stumps; metaphor becomes as natural as seeing, and as convincing.

The progression of nouns in the last stanzas there-fore needs no additional machinery of language to give it coherence, for these images—thread, scrawl, page, pyramid—are already metaphors of more than one di-mension even though their formation appears to be instantaneous and neural. The thread, we may say, is a thin beam of shadow; but shadow here is itself a metaphor for imagination, the very imagination which sees in the shadow a thread! What raises the poetry of Stevens to an unusual degree of excellence is his cognizance of all the intricacies of his own imagination.

164

He displays it and comments on it simultaneously. His fragments do not "represent" perceptions, nor do they form simple and self-explanatory metaphors. They embody an aesthetic process, and perhaps an individual sensibility—one with philosophical implications which the poet states in the last line of the poem.

In the preceding pages I have tried to suggest how the analysis of syntax may help a reader to understand individual poems. Such analysis, of course, should not supplant but merely supplement the study of vocabulary and prosody. Ideally, one reads with undivided attention to all these elements of poetry, but appreciating many modern poems requires considerable reflection on the various meanings of words and the multiple potential relations among them. It is important that a reader approach this poetry without too rigid preconceptions regarding the way a sentence "ought" to be constructed. He must be willing to allow finite verbs to function as nouns, or conjunctions to act as adjectives; he must read some noun phrases as belonging only "to a degree" in a sentence or as functioning simultaneously in two sentences. At times, he may also profit by meditating on his responses to a passage in the light of an examination of its disposition of grammatical elements, irreproachably orthodox as this disposition may be according to the traditional rules of the language. Doubtless any attempt to evaluate these responses in terms of four simple classifications of syntactic structures is doomed to inaccuracy and incompleteness. Nevertheless, evidence that merely suggests a relation between language and emotional response may serve to stimulate the development of more exact methods of defining that relation.

Summary

THE RESULTS of this inquiry indicate that the study of syntax can yield clear evidence of changes in literary style over a certain span of time, and that an understanding of these changes in all their implications may improve our ability to interpret individual poems. Specifically, poets of the 1870s habitually vary sentences by rearranging the order of the parts or by elaborating them to extraordinary complexity, while poets in the early twentieth century write a greater number of regular sentences and fragments of sentences. And poets use these kinds of structures for specific purposes; that is, syntax has an esthetic function in verse.

In early chapters I have described the nature and use in poetry of each kind of syntactic variation (elaboration, dislocation, fragmentation) as well as of the normal sentence pattern, and have traced the interrelations, synchronic and diachronic, among these kinds of structure. Then I have studied selected poems of W. B. Yeats, Gerard Manley Hopkins, T. S. Eliot, and Robert Browning in order to delineate the origin, range, and effect of modern poetic syntax. An analysis of samples from Yeats and Hopkins underscores the radical differences between individual styles which nevertheless share in the development of a new kind of poetry. These samples also illustrate the bearing of syntax on the question of "difficulty" or "obscurity" in poetry. Lines from Browning, on the other hand, have

166

an unmistakable kinship with passages from Eliot, so that certain typically modern structures are seen to have their origin in earlier poets.

Finally, I have speculated on the implications of this stylistic change and how it may affect our reading of poetry. The modern preference for regular and fragmentary structures has been related to the rise of democratic societies and to the emergence of new conceptions of reality based on new conceptions of the mind; and then, in the final chapter, the syntax of a few selected poems by recent authors has been examined to illustrate how sentence structure works integrally in a poem to produce certain definite effects. In an Auden poem, elaboration reinforces irony; in selections from Stevens, fragments achieve fidelity to the intricate movements of an individual imagination. By adapting syntax to enhance irony and to render inner reality, poets provide harmonious forms for the dominant themes of modern literature.

Appendix 1

SYNTACTIC STRUCTURES IN POETRY

THE "STATISTICS" in this appendix have a perhaps misleading appearance of rigorous exactitude. As I have explained in the introduction, my definitions of these three variations from normal word order do not encompass every structure which might appear to readers as somehow irregular. There are also ambiguous structures, impossible to identify with certitude as dislocations rather than fragments, fragments rather than phrases in a regular sentence. I know of no way to assign numerical values to ambiguities. Anyone who tries to duplicate my analysis is likely to categorize some doubtful cases differently, and his totals will vary from mine correspondingly. The number of such cases is so small, however, that I would not expect any significant change in the *proportion* of these variations to one another. When research assistants have analyzed the same samples using my general criteria, there have been few deviations of more than two or three units. The figures in this appendix, then, should be thought of as approximations, not precise quantities.

Poet	Number of Lines	Regular	Dislocated	Elaborate	Fragmentary	Dominant Types
Bryant (1794)	499	129	29	19 [1f, 2^2]	8 [3X]	DE: .23, .15
Emerson (1803)	497	178	33	19 [1f, 2^2]	34 [5X]	FD: .19, .19
Longfellow (1807)	504	100	129	11 [1^2]	27 [20X]	DF: 1.3, .27
Tennyson (1809)	525	268	69	11 [1^2]	216 [49X, 28c]	FD: .81, .26
Browning (1812)	498	80	63	31 [10^2, 3^3, 1^4]	80 [2c, 3x]	FD: 1.0, .79
Lowell (1819)	527	111	87	19 [1^2, 1^3]	19 [4X]	DE: .78, .17
Whitman (1819)	514	155	67	29 [2f, 1^5, 2^4, 1^3, 9^2, $2f^2$]	245 [62X, 4c]	FD: 1.6, .43
Arnold (1822)	508	152	76	15 [2^2]	15 [8X]	DE: .5, .09
Rossetti (1828)	528	107	60	22 [2^2]	40 [5X, 2c]	DF: .56, .37
Dickinson (1830)	504	142	38	11 [3^2]	46 [9X]	FD: .32, .27
Morris (1834)	492	146	90	32 [1f, 1^2]	25 [10X, 1c]	DE: .62, .22
Swinburne (1837)	495	88	55	43 [7^2, 1^3]	16 [1X]	$\frac{D}{E}$: .57, .50
Hardy (1840)	493	144	40	18 [1^2, 1^3]	5 [2c]	DE: .28, .12
Hopkins (1844)	496	144	89	18 [1f]	115 [17X, 7c]	FD: .80, .62

Wilde (1856)	492	169	28	13 [1^2, 1f]	45 [29X, 1c]	FD: .27, .17
Yeats (1865)	500	114	20	27 [1f]	16 [3X, 1c]	ED: .24, .17
Robinson (1869)	510	78	35	44 [4^2, 2f]	5 [3c]	ED: .56, .45
Frost (1875)	494	191	18	20	22 [1x, 3c]	FE: .11, .10
Sandburg (1878)	499	235	7	26 [1^5, 1^4, 1^3, 2^2, 1f]	72 [1c]	FE: .31, .11
Stevens (1879)	512	216	10	16 [2f, 1^2]	123 [1X, 12c]	FE: .57, .08
Williams (1883)	504	110	9	7 [1f]	109 [7X]	FD: 1.0, .11
Lawrence (1885)	522	172	6	21 [6f, $1f^2$, 1^2]	174	FE: 1.0, .12
Pound (1885)	502	133	22	5 [3f]	207 [2X, 5c]	FD: 1.6, .16
H. D. (1886)	530	104	23	14 [2^2, 1^3]	89 [1X, 15c]	FD: .86, .22
Eliot (1888)	496	173	20	14 [1^2, 1f]	70 [2c]	FD: .41, .11
Cummings (1894)	514	106	69	20 [7^2]	57 [3c]	DF: .65, .54
Graves (1895)	507	120	39	16 [2f]	69 [3X, 3c]	FD: .57, .33
Crane (1899)	515	151	42	14 [2f, 2^2]	97 [15X, 4c]	FD: .64, .27
Auden (1907)	512	107	14	24 [5f, 3^2]	47	FE: .44, .22
Thomas (1914)	491	149	30	25 [2^2, 3f]	88	FD: .59, .20

Note: f = "fragmentary" structure
c = colloquial fragment
x = exclamatory fragment

$X^{2, 3, 4 \ldots n}$ = number of (double, triple, quadruple . . . etc.) elaborations within a single structure

Appendix 2

Arnold, Matthew
"Dover Beach," "The Buried Life," "Rugby Chapel,"
"Westminster Abbey"
Auden, W. Hugh
"A Bride in the '30's," "At the Grave of H. J.," "In Sickness
and in Health," "1929"
Browning, Robert
First lines of *The Ring and the Book*
Bryant, William C.
"The Fountain," "Inscription to a Wood," "Monument
Mountain," "Song of the Sower"
Crane, Hart
"Cape Hatteras," "Rip Van Winkle," "The River," "The
Harbor Dawn," "To Brooklyn Bridge," "Southern Cross"
Cummings, E. E.
"Four" and "Five" from *Is 5*, except No. XII of "Four"
and no. II of "Five"; Nos. 192 to 200 of *W*, except nos.
197, 198.
Dickinson, Emily
Nos. I through XXXIII of *Nature*, except no. X
Eliot, T. S.
The Waste Land, "The Hollow Men," "Gerontion"
Emerson, Ralph W.
"Adirondacks," "Boston," "The Solution"
Frost, Robert

"The Bear," "The Grindstone," "New Hampshire"
Graves, Robert
"A Country Mansion," "The Eremites," "Halls of Bedlam,"
"The Great-Grandmother," "A Jealous Man," "Ogres and
Pigmies," "Recalling War," "The Terraced Valley," "To
the Sovereign Muse," "To Walk on Hills," "Saint," "The
Witches Cauldron"
H. D.
"Demeter," "Circe," "Charioteer," "Telesila"
Hardy, Thomas
"At the Pyramid of Cestius . . . ," "At Waking," "At A
Seaside Town in 1869," "A Young Man's Exhortation,"
"The Bridge of Lodi," "The Dance at the Phoenix,"
"Ditty," "Neutral Tones," "The Two Men"
Hopkins, Gerard M.
The Wreck of the Deutschland, "The Loss of the Eury-
dice," "The Bugler's First Communion," "The Nightingale"
Lawrence, D. H.
"Evening Land," "The Fish," "Manifesto," "Tortoise Shout"
Longfellow, Henry W.
First lines of *Evangeline* and *Hiawatha*, "Epimetheus,"
"The Lighthouse," "Prometheus," "Resignation"
Lowell, James R.
"Bankside," "l'Envoi," "Footpath," "Ode"
Morris, William
"Author to the Reader," "Gunnar's Howe," "Message of
the March Wind," "The Months," first lines of *Ogier the
Dane.*
Pound, Ezra
Hugh Selwyn Mauberley, except stanza XII, and "l'Envoi,"
stanza IV and "Medallion" from "Mauberley"; *Cantos* II,
III, IV
Robinson, Edward A.
"Man Against the Sky," "The Prodigal Son," "The Valley
of the Shadow," "The Wandering Jew"
Rossetti, Dante G.
"Burden of Nineveh," "Southsay," "The Stream's Secret"
Sandburg, Carl
"Haze," "Smoke and Steel," "The Windy City"
Stevens, Wallace
"The Man With The Blue Guitar," "Le Monocle de Mon
Oncle"

Swinburne, Algernon C.
"Ballad of Death," "Prelude," "Ave Atque Vale"
Tennyson, Alfred
"Charge of the Heavy Brigade," "Defense of Lucknow,"
"Locksley Hall Sixty Years After," "On the Jubilee . . ."
Thomas, Dylan
"Before I Knocked," "Ballad of the Long-Legged Bait,"
"I, In My Intricate Image," "In Country Sleep"
Whitman, Walt
"Memories of President Lincoln," "Passage to India," "The
Singer in the Prison"
Wilde, Oscar
"Athanasia," "The New Helen," "Ravenna"
Williams, William C.
"Della Primavera Trasportata Al Morale," "The Descent
of Winter," "March"
Yeats, William B.
"Among School Children," "The Dawn," "In Memory of
Major Robert Gregory," "Nineteen Hundred and Nine-
teen," "The Tower"

NOTE ON THE TEXTS

With a few exceptions, I chose texts for analysis according
to two criteria: it was necessary to take poems from reliable
editions; on the other hand, it was desirable to work on
texts which could be penciled at will. Whenever possible,
therefore, I took cheap editions from reputable presses in
preference to variorum, or "critical," or "authoritative"
editions.

In the case of nineteenth-century poets, there is no particular risk in using an inexpensive reprint of the final edition
seen through the press by the author; whatever errors es-
cape him are usually self-evident and removed in subsequent printings. Given the dearth of bibliographical information about most of these authors, however, I had to
assume that they made no or few changes in poems allegedly
written around 1870, but most readily available to me in
volumes published much later.

Hopkins, Whitman, and Dickinson were obvious exceptions. There is of course no nineteenth-century edition of
Hopkins' work, so the text prepared by Gardner for Oxford

175

in 1948 is accepted as the safe one. It is well known that Whitman tinkered with *Leaves of Grass* constantly, and, indeed, using the 1871 version of the poems instead of the 1902 text produces eight additional fragments. Dickinson poses a special problem. Johnson's accurate edition of her poems yields many more ambiguous constructions than the earlier "emended" versions. This edition restores the poet's dashes, which often make it difficult to decide whether a group of nouns is to be taken as a series of appositive phrases or as a series of fragments.

In the case of the twentieth-century poets, matters were simpler. I relied for the most part on editions first published around 1930. All of these were presumably seen through the press by the authors and are therefore reliable. Stevens, Auden, and Thomas did not collect their major work into handy, single volumes until the 1940s or 1950s, and so, again, I have assumed for my own convenience that no substantive changes were made in the poems after their first appearance. It was never my intention, however, to strive for a rigorously synchronic grouping, the important thing was to distinguish two generations of writers, one active before 1900, the other after.

Notes

INTRODUCTION

[1] Roman Jakobson, "Closing Statement: Linguistics and Poetics," *Style in Language,* eds. Sol Saporta and Thomas A. Sebeok (New York: M.I.T. Press and John Wiley and Sons, 1960), p. 377.

[2] M. A. K. Halliday, "Categories of the Theory of Grammar," *Word,* XVII, No. 3 (December 1961), 241–292. See also nn. 7 and 10, Chapter I.

[3] See especially "Part Three: Grammar" and "Part Five: Style and Stylistics" in *Essays on the Language of Literature,* eds. Seymour Chatman and Samuel R. Levin (Boston: Houghton, Mifflin, 1967). The article by W. Nelson Francis, "Syntax and Literary Interpretation," is of particular interest because it applies linguistic method to a modern poem as the preliminary to critical evaluation. In the same volume Richard Ohmann's "Literature as Sentences" treats deviant structures as one key to an author's aesthetic purposes. See also n. 12.

[4] Cf. Pallister Barkas, *A Critique of Modern English Prosody,* Studien zur englischen Philologie, no. 82 (Halle: Niemeyer, 1934); P. F. Baum, *The Principles of English Versification,* (Cambridge: Harvard University Press, 1922); George R. Stewart, *The Technique of English Verse* (New York: Kennikat Press, 1930); more recently, Karl Shapiro and Robert Beum, *A Prosody Handbook* (New York: Harper and Row, 1965).

[5] See, for example, Thomas Quale, *Poetic Diction: A Study of Eighteenth Century Verse* (London: Methuen and Co., 1924); Owen Barfield, *Poetic Diction: A study in Meaning* (London: Faber and Gwyer, 1925); Vere L. Rubel, *Poetic Diction of the Renaissance* . . . (New York: Oxford University Press, 1941); Josephine Miles, *The Vocabulary of Poetry* (Berkeley: University of California Press, 1946) and *The Continuity of Poetic Language* (Berkeley: University of California Press, 1951); Donald Davie, *Purity of Diction in English Verse* (London: Chatto and Windus, 1952); Bernard Groom, *The Diction of Poetry from Spenser to Bridges* (Toronto: University of Toronto Press, 1955).

177

[6] Jakobson, p. 375. See also nn. 7 and 23. However, Mats Redin, in *Word-Order in English Verse from Pope to Sassoon,* (Upsala: Upsala Universitets Arsskrift, 1925), has compiled a good deal of empirical evidence for the shift from much to little "dislocation" over two centuries. He does not pretend, however, to make his research directly pertinent to literary study: "My book contains masses of examples and many dull figures, but very little that throws light upon the psychology of verse-order. And surely that is the kernel of the whole question . . . analysis should have as its aim, not to collect instances of chiasmus, parallelism, or the like—which I consider less interesting, since such things occur in prose as well—but to scrutinize the deviations from prose-order with a view to ascertain their poetic effect" (p. 218).

[7] "But the problems of syntax in its poetic—and, in our case rhythmic—functions are almost untouched by research . . . although they involve linguistic elements no less than the number of stresses." Benjamin Hrushovski, "On Free Rhythms in Modern Poetry," *Style in Language,* ed. Sol Saporta and Thomas A. Sebeok, p. 179.

[8] Edward Sapir makes this assumption in *Language* (New York: Harcourt, Brace and Co., 1921), p. 242. I know of no one who has disputed it.

[9] Donald Davie, *Articulate Energy* (London: Routledge and Kegan Paul, 1955), p. vii.

[10] Francis Berry, *Poet's Grammar* (London: Routledge and Kegan Paul, 1958); Christine Brooke-Rose, *A Grammar of Metaphor* (London: Secker and Warburg, 1958); George Rostrevor Hamilton, *The Tell-Tale Article* (New York: Oxford University Press, 1950). Hamilton makes passing remarks about the "decay" of syntax in modern verse and its obsession with noun fragments; my research largely substantiates these insights.

[11] Samuel R. Levin, "Linguistic Structures in Poetry," *Janua Linguarum,* XXIII (Hague, 1962).

[12] Nicolas Ruwet, "L'Analyse structurale de la poésie," *Linguistics,* No. 2 (December 1963), 38–59. See also "Analyse structurale d'un poème français: un sonnet de Louise Labé," *Linguistics,* No. 3 (January 1964).

[13] A modern poem in free verse may, of course, have a highly effective, deliberately imposed metrical pattern; but such a pattern is likely to be an intrinsic property of a particular poem, highly asymmetric and not readily transferable.

[14] Wallace Fowlie, *Mid-Century French Poets* (New York: Grove Press, 1955), p. 33. Frederick Pottle, *The Idiom of Poetry* (New York: Cornell University Press, 1941), pp. 96 ff.; Herbert Read, *Phases of English Poetry* (Norfolk, Conn., 1951), pp. 48 ff.

[15] Louise Bogan, *Achievement in American Poetry* (New York: Gateway Editions, Inc., 1951), p. 85.

[16] Bogan, p. 65.

[17] Elizabeth Drew, *Directions in Modern Poetry* (New York: W. W. Norton and Co., 1952), p. 204.

[18] Babette Deutsch, *Poetry in Our Time* (New York: Henry Holt and Co., 1952), p. 151.

[19] Jacob Isaacs, *The Background of Modern Poetry* (New York: E. P. Dutton and Co., 1952), p. 20.

[20] T. S. Eliot, *Selected Essays* (New York: Harcourt, Brace, and Co., 1932), p. 248.

[21] John Crowe Ransom, "The Poetry of 1900–1950," *Kenyon Review*, XIII, No. 3 (Summer 1951), 449.

[22] Robinson Jeffers, "Poetry and Survival," *Perspectives, U.S.A.* (New York, 1953), p. 103.

[23] John Press, *The Chequer'd Shade* (New York: Oxford University Press, 1958), pp. 14–15.

[24] Helen Gardner, *The Art of T. S. Eliot* (New York: E. P. Dutton and Co., 1950), p. 71.

[25] F. O. Matthiessen, *The Achievement of T. S. Eliot* (New York: Oxford University Press, 1958), p. 15.

CHAPTER 1.

[1] William Cullen Bryant, *Poems* (New York, 1875), p. 213. (N.B.: Hereafter, references to works by poets listed on the chart in Appendix I are in the most cursory fashion possible; these references appear as shortened versions of the complete bibliographical references given in part I of the bibliography.)

[2] Bryant, "Green River," p. 30.

[3] Bryant, "The Song of the Sower," pp. 280–281.

[4] Pound, *Cantos*, II, ll. 6–8.

[5] Such assumptions are discussed in Leonard Bloomfield's "A Set of Postulates . . . ," *Readings in Linguistics*, ed. Martin Joos, American Council of Learned Societies (New York, 1958), p. 28.

[6] These terms were suggested to me by Miss Josephine Miles.

[7] Zellig Harris, "Co-occurrence and Transformation in Linguistic Structure," *The Structure of Language*, ed. Jerry A. Fodor and Jerrold J. Katz (Englewood Cliffs: Prentice-Hall, 1964), p. 156. Archibald Hill, *Introduction to Linguistic Structures* (New York: Harcourt, Brace and Co., 1958), p. 5. Edward Sapir, *Language* (New York: Harcourt, Brace and Co., 1921), p. 88.

[8] Bloomfield, *Language* (New York: Henry Holt and Company, 1933), p. 185.

[9] Hill, p. 262.

[10] Noam Chomsky, *Syntactic Structures* (Hague: Mouton and Co., 1957), p. 26.

[11] Charles C. Fries, *The Structure of English* (New York: Harcourt, Brace and Co., 1952), pp. 144 ff.

[12] Bloomfield, *Language*, p. 170.

[13] Fries, p. 213; W. Nelson Francis, *The Structure of American English* (New York: Ronald Press Co., 1958), 320–323.

[14] Hill, p. 237.

[15] Edward Stankiewicz, "Linguistics and the Study of Poetic Language," *Style in Language* (New York, 1960), p. 70.

[16] Stankiewicz, p. 84.

[17] Saporta and Chomsky have offered a more concrete notion of such a system. Saporta states, "Thus a sentence that violates a very general rule may be said to be less grammatical than a sentence that

violates only a more specific rule" (Sol Saporta, *Style in Language,* p. 92). Chomsky very briefly outlines a system of "categories" ranging from the finished sentence to the smallest units which a grammar is designed to generate, and determines degree of grammaticalness according to the level of specificity of structural description beyond which the grammar will not generate a given sequence (Chomsky, "Degrees of Grammaticalness," *The Structure of Language,* eds. Fodor and Katz, p. 387). A separate "grammar" for poetry, perhaps linked to that for the whole language through some transvaluation procedure, might adopt Chomsky's general notion of "categories" and "levels," as well as his cursive script.

[18] M. A. K. Halliday, "The Linguistic Study of Literary Texts," *Ninth Congress Papers,* Vol. XII of Janua Linguarum (Hague: Mouton and Co., 1962), p. 303.

CHAPTER 2.

[1] Longfellow, p. 229.
[2] Bryant, p. 27.
[3] Longfellow, p. 91.
[4] Browning, p. 650.
[5] Browning, p. 652.
[6] Browning, p. 651.
[7] Browning, p. 752.
[8] See Charles Fries, *The Structure of English* (New York: Harcourt, Brace and Co., 1952), where transcripts of actual conversations are given.
[9] Lawrence, *Poems,* p. 463.
[10] Cummings, "W," *Poems,* p. 229.
[11] Cummings, *Is 5,* p. 106.
[12] Cummings, *Is 5,* p. 92.
[13] Cummings , "W," *Poems,* p. 238.
[14] Bryant, pp. 280–281.
[15] Swinburne, "Ballad of Death," p. 19.
[16] Arnold, pp. 414–415.
[17] Tennyson, p. 471.
[18] Swinburne, p. 19.
[19] Tennyson, p. 519.
[20] Tennyson, p. 518.
[21] Tennyson, p. 471.
[22] Tennyson, p. 518.

CHAPTER 3.

[1] Pound, Canto IV, ll. 34–52.
[2] Pound, Canto IV, ll. 12–14.
[3] Pound, *Letters* (to W. C. Williams, December 19, 1913), p. 28.
[4] Pound, *Letters* (to Harriet Monroe, January, 1915), p. 49.
[5] Pound, *Letters,* p. 49.
[6] Swinburne, "Ave Atque Vale," p. 235.
[7] Whitman, p. 26.
[8] Whitman, p. 155.

[9] Lawrence, "Tortoise Shout," *Collected Poems*, p. 463.
[10] Sandburg, "Chicago," p. 3.
[11] Sandburg, from *Slabs of the Sunburnt West*, p. 312.
[12] Whitman, "Memories of President Lincoln," p. 302.
[13] Pound, *Hugh Selwyn Mauberley*, X, ll. 1–5.
[14] Eliot, p. 43.
[15] Eliot, p. 39.
[16] Crane, "Cape Hatteras," p. 37.
[17] Crane, "The River," p. 13.
[18] Scott, "Lay of the Last Ministrel," I, X, ll. 94–96.
[19] Browning, pp. 649–650.
[20] Morris, pp. 115–116.
[21] James Oppenheim, "The Lincoln Child," in Louis Untermeyer's *Modern American Poetry* (New York: Harcourt, Brace & Co., 1930), p. 354.
[22] Edith M. Thomas, "Frost Tonight," in Untermeyer, p. 112.
[23] Graves, "The Halls of Bedlam," p. 161.
[24] Frost, *Collected Poems*, p. 157.
[25] Wilde, p. 150.
[26] Untermeyer, p. 33.
[27] Thomas Parkinson, *W. B. Yeats, Self-Critic* (Berkeley and Los Angeles: University of California Press, 1951), pp. 33–35.
[28] See Lawrence's plea for a "stark, bare, rocky directness of statement" in a letter to Catherine Carswell, January 11, 1916, in *The Letters of D. H. Lawrence*, ed. Aldous Huxley (New York: Viking Press, 1932), p. 313.

CHAPTER 4.

[1] Hopkins, *Poems*, p. 63.
[2] Yeats, *Collected Poems*, p. 144.
[3] Hopkins, *Poems*, p. 66.
[4] *Poems and Prose of Gerard Manley Hopkins*, ed. W. H. Gardner (Baltimore: Penguin Books, 1953), p. 11.
[5] Hopkins, *Poems*, p. 66.
[6] Hopkins, *Poems*, p. 87.
[7] Letter quoted in *Poems and Prose of Gerald Manley Hopkins*, ed. W. H. Gardner (Baltimore: Penguin Books, 1953), p. 236.
[8] *Poems and Prose*, p. 236.
[9] Yeats, p. 192.
[10] Yeats, p. 194.
[11] John Unterecker, *A Reader's Guide to William Butler Yeats* (New York: Noonday Press, 1959), p. 176.

CHAPTER 5.

[1] Hilda Dale, *La Poésie française en Angleterre: 1850–1890* (Paris: Librairie Marcel Didier, 1954), pp. 41 ff., 91 ff.
[2] Dale, p. 52.
[3] René Taupin, *L'Influence du symbolisme française sur la poésie*

américaine (Paris: Librairie Ancienne Honore Champion, 1929), pp. 272 ff.

⁴ See articles by F. S. Flint and Pound in *Poetry*, I, No. 6 (March 1913), 199–206.

⁵ Taupin, p. 84.

⁶ Taupin, p. 92.

⁷ Marcel Raymond, *From Baudelaire to Surrealism*, trans. G. M. Wittenborn, Schultz (New York, 1949), pp. 61–62.

⁸ Taupin, p. 112.

⁹ Raymond, p. 258.

¹⁰ Raymond, p. 125.

¹¹ Taupin, p. 164.

¹² See H. R. Hays, "Surrealist Influence in Contemporary English and American Poetry," *Poetry*, LIV (July 1939), 202–209.

¹³ Quoted by Shapiro (see following note), p. 90.

¹⁴ Karl Shapiro, "English Prosody and Modern Poetry," *ELH*, XIV, No. 2 (June 1949), 78.

¹⁵ Otto Jespersen, *Growth and Structure of the English Language* (New York: Doubleday Anchor, 1956), p. 11.

¹⁶ Edward Sapir, *Language* (New York: Harcourt, Brace & Co., 1921), p. 166.

¹⁷ Letter to Louis Untermeyer from Amherst, Mass., Oct. 15, 1919. In *The Letters of Robert Frost to Louis Untermeyer* (New York: Holt, Rinehart and Winston, 1963).

¹⁸ See report on early reviews in chapter 5 of Elizabeth S. Sergeant's *Frost: The Trial by Existence* (New York: Holt, Rinehart and Winston, 1960), pp. 93–122. Such praise persists; see Reuben A. Brower, *The Poetry of Robert Frost* (New York: Oxford University Press, 1963), pp. 9 ff.

¹⁹ Letter to H. J. C. Grierson, Feb. 21 1926, in *The Letters of William Butler Yeats*, ed. Allan Wade (London: Rupert Hart-Davis, 1954), p. 710.

²⁰ Copy forwarded to Harriet Monroe of Williams' letter to R. P. Blackmur, dated Nov. 11, 1940. In *Harriet Monroe Papers*, Special Collections, University of Chicago Library.

²¹ Jespersen, p. 245.

²² The impact of the popular press and the technology of communication in general on the English language, in all its forms, is discussed in Heinrich Spies' *Kultur und Sprache in Neuen England* (Berlin: B. G. Teubner, 1928), pp. 50, 117.

²³ Shapiro, p. 91. This critic notes the correspondences between *vers libre* and prose, echoing John Livingston Lowes, who had made the observation 40 years earlier in *Convention and Revolt in Poetry* (Boston: Cambridge University Press, 1909), p. 280.

²⁴ Raymond, p. 66.

²⁵ Drew, *Directions in Modern Poetry* (New York: W. W. Norton and Co., 1952), pp. 266–267.

²⁶ Pound, "A Pact," *Selected Poems*, p. 27.

²⁷ Stevens, opening of "Thirteen Ways of Looking at a Blackbird," *Collected Poems*, p. 92.

[28] André Breton, *Poètes d'aujourd'hui 18* (Paris: Pierre Seghers, 1955), p. 150. First lines of "Pleine Marge."

[29] Babette Deutsch, *Poetry in our Time* (New York: Henry Holt and Co., 1952), p. 121.

[30] Cummings, *Poems,* p. 113.

[31] Deutsch, p. 50.

[32] Bogan, *Achievement in American Poetry* (New York: Gateway Editions, 1951), p. 17. Bogan's estimate of Sandburg's style also parallels that of Deutsch; see p. 42 of *Achievement.*

[33] Herbert Read, "The Drift of Modern Poetry," *Encounter,* IV, No. 1 (January 1955), p. 6.

[34] Stevens, *Collected Poems,* pp. 180, 182.

[35] Lawrence, *Poems,* p. 427.

[36] Ben W. Fuson, "The Poet and his Mask," *Park College Faculty Lectures* (Parkville, Mo.: Park College Press, 1954), p. 22.

[37] Fuson, p. 22.

[38] Fuson, p. 14.

[39] Fuson, p. 25.

[40] L. S. Vygotsky, *Thought and Language* (Cambridge: M.I.T. Press, 1962), pp. 119 ff., argues that "inner speech" is *qualitatively* different from uttered monologue. He establishes the characteristics of this "inner speech" by recording the "egocentric speech" of children—their "thinking aloud." His results are interesting in connection with this study because he finds evidence that inner speech is "disconnected and incomplete" (p. 139).

[41] Taupin, p. 114.

[42] Raymond, p. 234.

[43] Raymond, p. 290.

[44] Edmund Wilson, *Axel's Castle* (New York: Charles Scribner's Sons, 1931), p. 108.

[45] Albert Mordell, *The Literature of Ecstasy* (London: Andrew Melrose, 1921), p. 117.

[46] Mordell, p. 117.

[47] Sapir, p. 224.

[48] Sigmund Freud, *Basic Writings,* trans. A. A. Brill (New York: Modern Library, 1938), p. 543.

[49] Frederick Clarke Prescott, *The Poetic Mind* (New York: Macmillan, 1922), p. 88.

[50] Mordell, p. 182.

[51] Mordell, p. 184.

[52] Taupin, p. 85.

[53] Donald Davie, *Articulate Energy* (London: Routledge & Kegan Paul, 1955), p. 13.

[54] Raymond, pp. 62–63.

[55] Davie, pp. 65 ff.

[56] Read, "The Drift of Modern Poetry," p. 7.

[57] Babette Deutsch, *Poetry in our Time* (New York: Henry Holt & Co., 1952), p. 81.

[58] Davie, pp. 35–36.

[59] Davie, p. 36.

[60] Henri Bergson, *Essaie sur les données immédiates de la conscience* (Paris: Ancienne Librairie Germer-Baillière et C¹ᵉ, 1889), p. 75.

[61] Bergson, p. 66.

[62] Bergson, p. 101.

[63] Bergson, p. 11.

[64] Cleanth Brooks, *Modern Poetry and the Tradition* (Chapel Hill: University of North Carolina Press, 1939), p. 71.

[65] Brooks, p. 74.

[66] Franklin Fearing, remarks in symposium "Language in Culture," *American Anthropologist,* ed. Harry Hoijer, LVI, p. 2, Memoir No. 79 (December 1954), 55, 62 et passim. Fearing here quotes Gardner Murphy and J. Hochberg, "Perceptual Development: Some Tentative Hypotheses," *Psychological Review* 58:332–349.

[67] Fearing takes this observation from Koffka (1935); work not identified.

[68] Fearing (see n. 66, above).

[69] Robert Redfield, "The Primitive World," *Proceedings of the American Philosophical Society,* XCVI (1952), pp. 32–36.

[70] Benjamin Lee Whorf, *Language, Thought, and Reality* (Cambridge: Technology Press, 1956), pp. 134 ff.

[71] Fearing, p. 71. *Cf.* Heinz Werner, *Comparative Psychology of Mental Development* (Chicago: Follet, 1948); and *On Expressive Language,* ed. Werner (Worcester: Clark University Press, 1955).

[72] Wayne Shumaker, *Literature and the Irrational* (Englewood: Prentice-Hall, 1960), p. 105.

[73] Ernst Cassirer, *Psychologie du langage* (Paris: Felix Alcan, 1933), p. 20.

[74] Cassirer, p. 23.

[75] Cassirer, p. 38.

[76] Freud, *Basic Writings,* pp. 320, 323.

[77] Freud, p. 341.

[78] Davie, p. 63.

[79] Lawrence's letter to Harriet Monroe, in *Harriet Monroe Papers,* Special Collection of University of Chicago Library, dated July 31, 1914, from Covent Garden, W.C., comments on the poem "Ballad of Another Ophelia."

[80] Susanne Langer in Werner's *On Expressive Language* (see n. 71, above), p. 6.

[81] T. S. Eliot, *Selected Essays* (New York: Harcourt, Brace and Co., 1932), p. 248.

[82] Wilson, *Axel's Castle,* pp. 21–22.

[83] Hermann Pongs, *Das Bild in der Dichtung* (Marburg: N.G. Elwertische, 1939), II, 1.

[84] Pongs, p. 3.

[85] Albert Einstein, *Out of My Later Years* (New York: Philosophical Library, 1950), pp. 59 ff.

[86] Paper delivered at the annual MLA conference, Palmer House, Chicago, December 27, 1963.

[87] Douglas Bush, *Science and English Poetry* (New York: Oxford Press, 1950), p. 95.

CHAPTER 6.

[1] Quoted from Untermeyer's *Modern American Poetry* (New York: Harcourt, Brace and Co., 1930), p. 78.

[2] Untermeyer, p. 417.

[3] Hardy, p. 511.

[4] Denise Levertov, "The Five Day Rain," *The New American Poetry*, ed. Donald Allen (New York: Grove Press, 1960), pp. 66–67.

[5] Pound, *Cantos*, p. 10.

[6] "A Farewell to Naples," *Blackwood's*, LXVII, No. 412 (February 1850), p. 279.

[7] Eliot, *Poems*, p. 49.

[8] Eliot, p. 47.

[9] Auden, *Collected Poetry*, p. 3.

[10] Pound, *Selected Poems*, p. 158.

[11] Williams, *Patterson*, III (New York: New Directions, 1949), p. 117.

[12] Auden, *Shorter Poems*, p. 151.

[13] Ginsberg, *The New American Poetry*, ed. Donald Allen, pp. 182–83.

[14] Stevens, *Selected Poems*, Vintage paperback, p. 57.

[15] Stevens, *Collected Poems*, p. 175.

[16] Stevens, *Collected Poems*, p. 459.

Bibliography

1. Sources of Material Drawn from Thirty Poets, 1870–1930

Arnold, Matthew. *Poetical Works.* New York: T. Y. Crowell, 1897.
Auden, W. H. *Collected Poetry.* New York: Random House, 1945.
———. *Collected Shorter Poems 1930–1944.* London: Faber & Faber, 1944.
Browning, Robert. *Complete Poetical Works.* New York: Macmillan, 1917.
Bryant, William Cullen. *Poems.* New York: Appleton, 1875.
Crane, Hart. *Collected Poems,* ed. Waldo Frank. New York: Liveright, 1933.
Cummings, E. E. *Poems, 1923–1954.* New York: Harcourt, Brace, 1954.
———. *Is 5.* New York: Horace Liveright, 1926.
Doolittle, Hilda. *Collected Poems.* New York: Boni and Liveright, 1925.
Dickinson, Emily. *The Poems of Emily Dickinson,* ed. Thomas H. Johnson. 3 vols. Cambridge: Harvard Press, 1955.
Eliot, T. S. *The Complete Poems and Plays.* New York: Harcourt, Brace, 1952.
Emerson, Ralph Waldo. *Poems.* Boston: Houghton, Mifflin, 1899.
Frost, Robert. *Collected Poems.* New York: Henry Holt, 1930.
———. *The Letters of Robert Frost to Louis Untermeyer.* New York: Holt, Rinehart, and Winston, 1963.
Graves, Robert. *Collected Poems.* London: Cassell and Co., 1938.
Hardy, Thomas. *Collected Poems.* New York: Macmillan, 1926.
Hopkins, Gerard Manley. *Poems.* New York: Oxford University Press, 1948.

————. *Poems and Prose.* London: Penguin Books, 1953.

Longfellow, Henry Wadsworth. *The Complete Poetical Works.* Boston: Houghton, Mifflin, 1902.

Lawrence, D. H. *Collected Poems.* II, New York: Jonathan Cape, 1929.

————. *Letters,* ed. Aldous Huxley. New York: Viking Press, 1932.

Lowell, James Russell. *Complete Poetical Works.* Boston: Houghton, Mifflin, 1896.

Morris, William. *The Poems of William Morris.* New York: Thomas Y. Crowell, 1904.

Pound, Ezra. *Cantos.* New York: New Directions, 1948.

————. *Letters (1907–1941).* New York: Harcourt, Brace, 1950.

————. *Personae.* New York: New Directions, 1926.

————. *Selected Poems.* New York: New Directions, 1957.

Robinson, Edwin Arlington. *Collected Poems.* New York: Macmillan, 1946.

Rossetti, Dante Gabriel. *Poems, Ballads and Sonnets.* New York: Doubleday Doran, 1937.

Sandburg, Carl. *Complete Poems.* New York: Harcourt, Brace, 1950.

Stevens, Wallace. *Collected Poems.* New York: Alfred A. Knopf, 1961.

————. *Selected Poems.* New York: Vintage Paperback, 1957.

Swinburne, Algernon Charles. *The Best of Swinburne,* ed. Clyde Kenneth Hyder and Lewis Chase. New York: Thomas Nelson and Sons, 1937.

Tennyson, Alfred Lord. *The Poetic and Dramatic Works of Alfred Lord Tennyson.* Boston: Houghton, Mifflin, 1898.

Thomas, Dylan. *Collected Poems.* New York: New Directions, 1953.

Whitman, Walt. *Leaves of Grass* ("Inclusive Edition"), ed. Emory Holloway. Garden City: Doubleday, 1926.

Wilde, Oscar. *Political Works.* New York: Thomas Y. Crowell, 1913.

Williams, William Carlos. *The Collected Earlier Poems.* New York: New Directions, 1938.

Yeats, William Butler. *Collected Poems.* New York: Macmillan, 1956.

————. *Letters,* ed. Allan Wade. London: Rupert Hart-Davis, 1954.

2. Selected Bibliography of Works Consulted

Allen, Donald M. *The New American Poetry*. New York, 1960.

Barry, Sister M. Martin. *An Analysis of the Prosodic Structure of Selected Poems of T. S. Eliot*. Washington, D.C., 1948.

Bergson, Henri. *Essai sur les donnés immédiates de la conscience*. Paris, 1889.

Berry, Francis. *Poet's Grammar*. London, 1958.

Blackmur, R. P. *The Double Agent*. New York, 1935.

Blair, Hugh. *Lectures on Rhetoric and Belles Lettres*. Philadelphia, 1860.

Blanchot, Maurice. "L'Écriture automatique, l'inspiration," *La Nouvelle NRF*, XVII, 3 (March 1953), 485–492.

Bloomfield, Leonard. *Language*. New York, 1933.

Bly, Robert. "On English and American Poetry," *The Fifties*, II (Briarwood Hill, 1959).

Bogan, Louise. *Achievement in American Poetry*. New York, 1951.

Bowra, C. M. *The Heritage of Symbolism*. London, 1943.

Breton, André. *Manifestes du surréalisme suivis de prolégomènes à un troisième manifeste de surréalism ou non*. Paris, 1946.

Brooke-Rose, Christine. *A Grammar of Metaphor*. London, 1958.

Brooks, Cleanth. *Modern Poetry and the Tradition*. Chapel Hill, 1939.

Brown, Roger. *Words and Things*. Glencoe, 1958.

Buhler, Charlotte. "Erfindung und Entdeckung," *Zeitschrift für Asthetik und Allgemeine Kunstwissenschaft*, XV, 1 (Stuttgart, 1920), 43–87.

Bush, Douglas. *Science and English Poetry*. New York, 1950.

Caillois, Roger. Introduction to *Anthologie de la poésie française moderne*. Buenos Aries, n.d.

Cassirer, Ernst. *Psychologie du langage*. Paris, 1933.

Chatman, Seymour and Samuel R. Levin, eds. *Essays on the Language of Literature*. Boston, 1967.

Chomsky, Noam. *Syntactic Structures*. Hague, 1957.

———. "Degrees of Grammaticalness." *The Structure of Language*, Englewood Cliffs, N.J., 1964, 384–389.

Clouard, Henri. *Histoire de la littérature française*. Paris, 1949.

Cox, Sidney. "Poetry and People," *Antioch Review*, IX, 4 (December 1949), 537–541.

Daiches, David. *Poetry and the Modern World*. Chicago, 1940.

Dale, Hilda. *La Poésie française en Angleterre*. Paris, 1954.

Davie, Donald. *Articulate Energy*. London, 1955.

188

Deutsch, Babette. *Poetry in Our Time*. New York, 1952.
Drew, Elizabeth. *Directions in Modern Poetry*. New York, 1952.
Eliot, T. S. *Ezra Pound, His Metric and Poetry*, New York, 1917.
————. *From Poe to Valéry*. New York, 1948.
————. *Selected Essays*. New York, 1932.
Enkvist, Nils Erik, John Spencer, and Michael Gregory. *Linguistics and Style*. London, 1964.
Fodor, Jerry A. and Ferrold J. Katz, eds. *The Structure of Language*. New Jersey, 1964.
Fraiberg, Louis. "Freud's Writings on Art," *Literature and Psychology*, MLA Newsletter, VI, 4 (November 1956),
Francis, W. Nelson. *The Structure of American English*. New York, 1958.
Freud, Sigmund. *Basic Writings*. New York, 1938.
Friar, Kimon and John Malcolm Brinnin, eds. *Modern Poetry: American and British*. New York, 1951.
Fries, Charles C. *The Structure of English*. New York, 1952.
Fuson, Ben. *The Poet and His Mask*. Parkville, Mo., 1954.
Goodman, Paul. "Advance-guard Writing, 1900–1950," *Kenyon Review*, XIII, 3 (Summer 1951), 357–380.
Graves, Robert. *Poetic Unreason*. London, 1925.
Halliday, M. A. K. "Categories of the Theory of Grammar," *Word*, XVII, No. 3 (December 1961), 241–292.
————. "The Linguistic Study of Literary Texts," *Ninth Congress Papers*. Vol. XII of Janua Linguarum. Hague: Mouton and Co., 1962.
Hamilton, George Rostrevor. *The Tell-Tale Article*. New York, 1950.
Hartman, Geoffrey. *The Unmediated Vision*. New Haven, 1954.
Hays, H. R. "Surrealist Influence in Contemporary English and American Poetry," *Poetry*, LIV (July 1939), 202–207.
Henrich, Edith. "Poetry as Communication," *The Pacific Spectator*, III, 2 (Spring 1949), 125–140.
Hill, Archibald. *Introduction to Linguistic Structures*. New York, 1958.
————. "A Program for the Definition of Literature," *University of Texas Studies in English*, XXVII (1958), 46–52.
Hill, J. C. "Poetry and the Unconscious," *British Journal of Medical Psychology*, IV, 2 (1924).
Hoijer, Harry, ed. "Language in Culture," *American Anthropologist*, LVI, 2, Memoir 79 (December 1954).
————. "Linguistic and Cultural Change," *Language*, XXIV (1948), 335–345.
Hoops, Reinald. *Der Einfluss der Psychoanalyse auf die englische Literatur*. Heidelberg, 1934.

Hughes, Glenn. *Imagism and the Imagists: A Study in Modern Poetry*. Palo Alto, 1931.

Isaacs, Jacob. *The Background of Modern Poetry*. New York, 1952.

Jakobson, Roman. "Closing Statement: Linguistics and Poetics," *Style in Language*. New York, 1960.

Jarrell, Randall. *Poetry and the Age*. New York, 1953.

Jeffers, Robinson. "Poetry and Survival," *Perspectives, U.S.A.*, New York, 1953, 102–107.

Jespersen, Otto. *Growth and Structure of the English Language*. New York, 1956 (first published, 1905).

Joos, Martin, ed. *Readings in Linguistics*. New York, 1958.

Kermode, Frank. *Romantic Image*. London, 1957.

Korg, Jacob. "Modern Art Techniques in *The Waste Land*," *JAEC*, XVIII, No. 4 (June 1960), 456–464.

Lawrence, D. H. *Sex, Literature and Censorship*. London, 1955.

Leavis, F. R. *New Bearings in English Poetry*. London, 1932.

Lemaître, Georges E. *From Cubism to Surrealism in French Literature*. Cambridge, 1941.

Levin, Samuel R. "Linguistic Structures in Poetry," *Janua Linguarum*, XXIII (1962).

———. "Poetry and Grammaticalness," *Ninth Congress Papers*, 308–315.

Lewis, C. Day. *The Poetic Image*. London, 1947.

Maritain, Jacques. *The Situation of Poetry*. New York, 1959.

Michaud, Guy. *Message poétique du symbolisme*. 4 vols., Paris, 1947.

Miles, Josephine. *The Continuity of Poetic Language*. Berkeley, 1951.

Miller, James E. "Four Cosmic Poets," *University of Kansas City Review*, XXIII, No. 4 (June 1957), 312–320.

Mizener, Arthur. "Some Notes on the Nature of English Poetry," *Sewanee Review*, LI (1943), 27–51.

Moore, George, ed. *An Anthology of Pure Poetry*. New York, 1925.

Mordell, Albert. *The Literature of Ecstasy*. London, 1921.

Morier, Henri. *Le Rythme du vers libre symboliste et ses relations avec le sens*. Genève, 1943.

Munson, Gorham. *Destinations*. New York, 1928.

Nida, Eugene A. *A Synopsis of English Syntax*. Norman, 1960.

O'Connor, William Van. *Sense and Sensibility in Modern Poetry*. Chicago, 1948.

Ohmann, Richard. "Literature as Sentences," *CE*, XXVII, No. 4 (January 1966), 261–267.

Pongs, Hermann. *Das Bild in der Dichtung*. 2 vols., Marburg, 1939.

Pottle, Frederick A. *The Idiom of Poetry*. New York, 1941.

Pound, Ezra. *Instigations of Ezra Pound*. New York, 1920.

———. *Polite Essays*. London, 1937.

Prescott, Frederick C. *The Poetic Mind*. New York, 1922.

Press, John. *The Chequer'd Shade*. New York, 1958.

———. *Rule and Energy*. New York, 1963.

Psychologie du langage. (Articles by Pongs, Cassirer, Meillet, Sapir, Jespersen, Bally) Paris, 1933.

Raiziss, Sona. *La Poésie américaine 'Moderniste' 1910–1940*. Paris, 1943.

Ransom, John Crowe. "The Poetry of 1900–1950," *Kenyon Review*, XIII, No. 3 (Summer 1951), 445–454.

Raymond, Marcel. *From Baudelaire to Surrealism*. New York, 1949.

Read, Herbert. *Phases of English Poetry*. Norfolk, Conn., 1951.

———. "The Drift of Modern Poetry," *Encounter*, IV, No. 1 (January 1955).

Redfield, Robert. "The Primitive World," *Proceedings of the American Philosophical Society*, XCVI (1952), 32–36.

Redin, Mats. *Word-Order in English Verse from Pope to Sassoon*. Upsala, 1925.

Reicke, Ilse. "Das Dichter in psychologischer Betrachtung," *Zeitschrift fur Asthetik und Allgemeine Kunstwissenschaft*, X, 1 (Stuttgart, 1915), 290–345.

Richards, I. A. *Principles of Literary Criticism*. New York, 1926.

Rosenthal, M. S. *The Modern Poets*. New York, 1960.

Ruwet, Nicholas. "Analyse structurale d'un poème français: un sonnet de Louise Labé," *Linguistics*, No. 3 (January 1964), 62–82.

———."L'Analyse structurale de la poésie," *Linguistics*, No. 2 (December 1963), 38–59.

Sapir, Edward. *Language*. New York, 1921.

Saporta, Sol and Thomas A. Sebeok, eds. *Style in Language*. New York, 1960.

Scudder, Vida. *The Life of the Spirit in the Modern English Poets*. Cambridge, 1895.

Shapiro, Karl. "English Prosody and Modern Poetry," *ELH*, XIV, No. 2 (June 1947), 77–92.

Shumaker, Wayne. *Literature and the Irrational*. Englewood, 1960.

Spier, Leslie A., Iriving Hallowell, and Stanley S. Newman, eds. *Language, Culture, and Personality*. Menasha, 1941.

191

Spies, Heinrich. *Kultur und Sprache im Neuen England*. Berlin, 1928.

Stankiewicz, Edward. "Linguistics and the Study of Poetic Language," in *Style in Language*. New York, 1960.

Stauffer, Donald A. *The Nature of Poetry*. New York, 1946.

Tate, Allen. *Reactionary Essays on Poetry and Ideas*. New York, 1936.

Taupin, René. *L'Influence du symbolisme français sur la poésie américaine*. Paris, 1929.

Vigée, Claude. "Metamorphoses of Modern Poetry," *Comparative Literature*, VII, No. 2 (Spring 1955), 97–120.

————. "L'Invention poétique et l'automatisme mental," *Modern Language Notes*, LXXV, No. 2 (February 1960), 143–154.

Vygotsky, Lev Semenovich. *Thought and Language*. Cambridge, 1962.

Warfel, Harry R. "Syntax Makes Literature," *CE*, XXI, No. 5 (February 1960), 251–55.

Werner, Heinz, ed. *On Expressive Language*. Worcester, 1955.

————. *Comparative Psychology of Mental Development*. Chicago, 1948.

————. *Die Ursprunge der Metapher*, 1919.

Whorf, Benjamin Lee. *Language, Thought, and Reality*, Cambridge, 1956.

Wilson, Edmund. *Axel's Castle*. New York, 1931.

Winters, Yvor. *In Defense of Reason*. New York, 1947.

Index

Cummings, E. E. (*continued*)
33-35; colloquialism of, 117;
mentioned, 2, 14, 26, 61, 107,
108, 115, 159

Daniel, Samuel, 121
Daudet, Alphonse, 126
Davie, Donald, on syntax, 6, 126-
128, 137
De Gourmont, Rémy, influence on
American poets, 109
Descriptive fragments in poetry,
153-155
Deutsch, Babette, 8, 128
Dickinson, Emily: everyday
speech in, 81; mentioned, 61,
112
Doolittle, Hilda, 77, 79, 110
Dramatic monologue: inclusion in
this study, 15; as interior mon-
ologue, 122-123
Drayton, Michael, 121
Dreams, relation to poetry, 134
Drew, Elizabeth, 8, 116

Eliot, George, 82
Eliot, T. S.: critics' comments on,
8-9; fused structures, 68-69; relation to Browning, 84, 99-100;
"hovering" fragments, 101-104;
ambiguity of fragments, 103-
104; French influence on, 108;
*The Love Song of J. Alfred
Prufrock,* 123; use of fragments, 154-155; mentioned, 6,
24, 37, 48, 66, 71, 75, 80, 82,
85, 90, 93, 109, 110, 112, 114,
115, 124, 137, 138
Emerson, R. W., 61, 78, 80, 81,
112, 126
Essay on Criticism, 126
Ezra, Moses Ibn, 126

Fearing, Franklin 131
Fenellosa, Ernest, 148; on Chi-
nese ideogram, 128
Fletcher, J., 111
Flint, 77
Fort, Paul, 109, 110
Fowlie, Wallace, 8

Fragmentation as means of representing mental life, 128
Francis, W. Nelson, on adjective
position, 21
French poetry: influence on English poetry, 109; psychic realism in, 123
Freud, Sigmund, 126, 136, 141
Fries, Charles: on subject-verb order, 19; on adjective position,
21
Frost, Robert: regularity of, 79-
80; colloquialism in, 115; mentioned, 37, 112, 118
Fuson, Ben, 121-122

Gardner, Helen, 9
Gautier, Théophile, 108
Ginsberg, Alan, 159
Gourmont, Rémy de. *See* De
Gourmont
Grammar: character and location
of words, 17; degrees of gram-
maticalness, 21; unorthodox,
158
Graves, Robert: fragments in, 76;
mentioned, 82, 115
Greeley, Horace, 71
Grierson, H. J. C., 112

H. D. (Hilda Doolittle), 77, 79,
110
Halliday, M. A. K., 5; on stylistics, 22
Hamilton, G. R., 6
Hardy, Thomas: syntactic patterns of, 150-151; as a novelist,
82; mentioned, 9, 79, 80, 81,
112
Harris, Zellig, 17-18
Hearn, Lafcadio, 126
Hemingway, Ernest, 82, 114
Heyward, DuBose, use of syntax,
144-150
Hill, Archibald, 17-18; on adverb
position, 21
Hopkins, Gerard Manley: as forerunner of modern poetry, 24,
84; concurrent dislocation and
elaboration, 85-86; fragmentation in, 86; obscurity of, 87-91;